EMPOWER
YOURSELF

EMPOWER YOURSELF

7 STEPS TO PERSONAL SUCCESS

JOHN MARTIN

SOUND WISDOM
P.O. Box 310
Shippensburg, PA 17257-0310

For more information on publishing and distribution rights, call 717-530-2122 or info@soundwisdom.com.

Quantity Sales. Special discounts are available on quantity purchases by corporations, associations, and others. For details, contact the Sales Department at Sound Wisdom.

ISBN 13 TP: 978-1-64095-047-4
ISBN 13 Ebook: 978-1-64095-048-1

For Worldwide Distribution, Printed in the U.S.A.
1 2 3 4 5 6 7 8 / 21 20 19 18

Cover/Jacket designer Eileen Rockwell
Interior design by Susan Ramundo

For Heather

CONTENTS

Traveler, there is no path; paths are made by walking.

—A SPANISH SAYING

PREFACE

I've chosen chapter titles to represent actions and ideas that can help you attain your definition of success.

While I promise you success if you apply to your own life the information contained within these pages, I do not guarantee a quick and easy journey. Self-discovery can be challenging. Growing a business, building a career, and reaching personal goals takes time, work, and dedication. But success is certain if you choose to push yourself out of your comfort zone, your routine, and your risk-free life.

What do you want your story to be? What would every day look like for you in the most ideal life you can imagine?

All we have is time, and it will pass regardless of what we do—how will you choose to spend it? And make no mistake, you are choosing. Some of us imagine by not making the difficult decisions about what we want in life that we are simply going with the flow, but the truth is, you choose your program or your program chooses you—meaning, if you don't intentionally choose the actions you take each day, you will take the path that your habits dictate. You'll be following a program either way.

The starting point is assessing yourself and being honest in looking at where you are and where you want to be. From there, the way forward is becoming self-aware—learning your strengths, weaknesses, and values. The next step is overcoming your fears, which will allow you to start seeing the world in a positive light. By being positive, you will dwell less on past mistakes and pain. All of this enables you to live in the present moment, discover and enjoy the work you do, and realize success.

The final step is to share with others. Each person communicates to the world in a unique way that is received by others in a unique way—you never know how your experience and knowledge can help another.

The internet and modern technology make it easy to share the ideas and practices that help you along your way to success.

Believe in yourself and share your passion with others. Believe that no matter what happens, you will come out OK. This is a confidence, a self-assuredness, that you carry through any situation you encounter in life. It's not "fake it till you make it." Authenticity is everything. If you don't believe in yourself above all else, everything you *do* and *say* loses its foundation and power.

From personal life to professional business, you have to know who you are, love and accept who you are, and believe in your abilities. You have to believe in your purpose, and if you enjoy what you are doing, your enthusiasm and confidence will show.

If you want to be free on the outside, the key is to be free on the inside. Many have observed that in order to be at peace with others, you have to be at peace with yourself. Our discontent has less to do with our job, colleagues, partner, or the amount of money we earn or accumulate, and more to do with how in tune we are with ourselves and our choices.

You can create the life you want one decision at a time, and it starts with the decision to look inside and be honest. Taking that courageous leap puts you on the right course, and it continues as you accept and act on what you learn about yourself. Eventually, you will join others who are on that road, facing the challenges of self-discovery, pushing through discomfort, and using the knowledge they gain to create and live the life they dreamed for themselves.

CHAPTER ONE

ASSESS YOUR LIFE

No self knowledge without self-confrontation;
no self-realization without self-knowledge.
—ANONYMOUS

To prepare for our journey of personal success, we need to evaluate exactly where we are in life and decide what it is or where it is that we would like to be. This is the starting point on our road to success. We begin by asking ourselves a series of questions. They don't have to be the ones I present here, but they should follow a similar line of questioning that you can answer honestly to get you to two basic points: one, an ultimate goal in life; and two, a fair determination of where you are right now in relation to that goal.

I call it an ultimate goal because its attainment will be the result of you setting and achieving success with smaller, related goals. An example of this might be getting your bachelor's, master's, and then doctorate degree with the ultimate goal of becoming a professor at a university. Another example would be going to barber school and cutting hair for a required number of hours to become a licensed barber while saving money to eventually reach your ultimate goal of owning your own barbershop. Another example would be researching an area that you love (maybe a particular city, state, or country) and finding a job and place to live with the ultimate goal of moving and establishing your home in that area.

Whatever it is, your ultimate goal should be big enough to be challenging, and the thought of it should inspire in you a sense of satisfaction or fulfillment.

So where are you now? Is this the job, industry, or relationship you want to be in? Maybe you're an entrepreneur and CEO of a company, and you'd rather be working in a supporting role so you could spend more time with your family. Maybe you work for a company and you would rather be operating your own. Maybe you simply do not enjoy what you do for a living. What would you rather be doing? Are you happy with your financial status? How much money would you like to have or earn? Are you living in the area you would like to live in? Where would you live if you could live anywhere?

Take a minute and write down your definition of success. Even if you've done this before, write down what comes to mind when you think of your success. Consider what your work, your primary relationships, and your overall lifestyle would look like. This is your ultimate goal.

Is it in line with what you are doing now? Is what you are doing taking you down the path that will lead to that lifestyle? These are things to consider as we move through this idea of self-assessment.

As we decide upon our ultimate goal, we have to clear away a road block that often stops people before they get started. We need to make sure that we are not blaming others for our current situation and accept personal responsibility for our lives. Even if there is a solid reason for blaming others for our circumstances, we should overcome this impulse and focus on owning our situation down to the minutia.

Even if you are right in pointing the finger, the outcome will not change, and you will not reach your goal or be able to see your goal if you're carrying resentment.

Accept Personal Responsibility

As you think about your current sources of discontent or disappointment in your life circumstances, notice what stands out in your mind and begin to dispose of your long-held excuses. What you are doing for a living is what you are choosing to do for a living. It's not your boss that is causing you to be miserable. You're not working with people you dislike because you have to "pay the bills." You're choosing to work there. When you cut away all the excuses, this is the cold truth that remains.

You're in the relationship you are in because that's the relationship you are choosing to be in. If you're miserable in that relationship, it's because you haven't taken the necessary steps to improve it, which may or may not include leaving it altogether. It's not because he won't go to counseling, or she drinks too much, or he is lazy, or she spends too much money, or that your mother-in-law is an insufferable old hag. It's because you made these choices.

It's not him or her or them or your childhood. It's only you. It's not the Democrats, Republicans, racists, or sexists that are responsible.

We have to let go of the excuses and own our lives—the good, bad, and ugly. If you are not where you want to be in your personal or professional life, it is your fault alone. The good news is that if your failures are your fault, then your success can come by the same method—your own choices.

Once you accept personal responsibility for your current circumstances in life, you are free to take the steps to change them.

Listen to Your Inner Voice

Let's get back to the first step in your journey—finding out what you want to do and where you want to go.

There is something in the back of your mind that you are interested in more than other things. There is an activity or a career that you are drawn to. Pay attention to this interest. Each of us is born with unique DNA, which means we have specific desires and interests and unique ways of communicating. When we start listening and following the inner voice that is special to us as an individual, we get closer to what we were meant to do.

How many of us drown out that inner voice by medicating ourselves with substances and distraction? When we medicate ourselves, we are trying to find a solution to feeling incomplete. Unfortunately, the reverse happens. We chase good times and good feelings to make us feel better about doing work that does not fulfill us, but when we come back to our day-to-day life—as of course we must—we feel more incomplete than ever.

If we are ignoring this DNA code in order to please our parents or a spouse or society or out of fear of money issues, we are more likely to be involved in negative habits or environments that hurt us because we are running from our true calling. We have to pay attention to the interests that lead us to explore various career fields or change careers or choose a goal in life even if that choice may not make sense to other people around us.

Here are two ways to start finding this inner voice even if you are currently blocking it out with your choices. The first is to recall your childhood and think of what you did that made you happy. What were some of your go-to activities? What were you good at? Secondly, take a look at what you consume. What kind of entertainment? What books do you like to read? What television shows do you like to watch? What do you read or watch online? What do you buy a lot?

Examining your life in this way can lead to the discovery of an interest that if pursued, could change your direction and give you renewed purpose.

There are too many people doing what their mother or father did because that's the way it always was. This breeds discontent. The discontent spreads and causes people to seek distractions and addictions and consumerism and anything that will keep them from facing the truth that they are choosing to live a life that they are not happy with.

Stephen Pressfield, in his book *The War of Art* puts it this way: "When we drug ourselves to blot out our soul's call, we are being good Americans and exemplary consumers. We're doing exactly what TV commercials and pop materialist culture have been brainwashing us to do from birth. Instead of applying self-knowledge, self-discipline, delayed gratification, and hard work, we simply consume a product."

Discover Why

Discovering your reason *why* is a critical step in this process of empowerment through evaluation.

It's important to start with *why* especially when it comes to the work that you do. Why do you do what you do for a living? It's an important question to answer. Did you just stumble into it? Are you doing it to pay the mortgage? Are you doing it because it's good money? Or do you believe in it? Are you helping people out by doing it? Are you making the world a better place? Do you quite simply just enjoy doing it? Did your parents push you into it?

Maybe they did. If you were brought up in a family business, you are in a position where you may not have seen the world full of choices. It may have been expected that you helped and eventually worked full time in the business. Your needs and wants were secondary to what put food on the table. If you find yourself in this situation, you may feel a sense of guilt about wanting to leave. When you decide what it is you would rather do, formulate a plan, and go.

Please, for the sake of yourself and others, be honest with yourself about why you're doing what you're doing for a living. It's critical to finding your starting point for personal success.

Maybe your why is simply to provide a better life for your family or to become more knowledgeable in a field of study. Maybe you are doing what you are doing for only a few years so that you can earn enough money to pay for additional education. Any reason why, as long as it is clear and can be communicated with positivity and authenticity, is a perfect starting point for selling your product or starting your business.

Learn and embrace your reason why. Hang onto it. It will strengthen you and help you both personally and professionally.

When we are acting from consistent, authentic, and clear motives, we are getting closer to doing that thing we were meant to do.

Prepare to Take Action

Whatever your desire and your reason for it, it will demand action on your part. It might be picking up extra shifts or finding ways to make bonus money at your job. It might be selling unwanted items from your house to make extra money. Maybe it means a lifestyle change like not eating out as much or going to the movies every weekend. It might be making that phone call that you've been putting off for so long or researching the steps to get you into a training program that would benefit you.

Many times self-assessment will reflect a need to make a significant change. It may be a change in company or even career and industry, or it may mean personal relationships need to change. Whatever the case, heed the call. Listen to that persistent voice, and pay attention to what you learn and to the signs around you.

In 1986, following his graduation from college, Jeff Bezos got a job in computer science on Wall Street. Shortly after, he worked in international trade with a company called Fitel and then worked at Banker's Trust for a time. Finally, he managed to land a position with a hedge fund company called D. E. Shaw & Co., also on Wall Street. Bezos worked hard, and by 1994 at the age of thirty, he was the youngest senior vice president in the history of the company, and it was clear that he would move up even higher in the ranks. But that same year, as a senior vice president making a comfortable six-figure salary, Jeff made a strange career choice.

He quit.

Jeff's real interest was in electronic retail. He was fascinated by the growing utility of the World Wide Web, and he wanted to spend more time learning and understanding how he could start his own retail business within this new technology. One day, while still working at D. E. Shaw, he came across the statistic that made him STOP, assess his life, and make a bold change. The statistic showed that internet usage was rising at a rate of 2,300% per month!

He knew he had to follow his calling. Bezos quit his job, packed up his family, and while moving across the country, typed up his business plan. A short time later, Amazon.com was born in the garage of a rented house in Seattle, and the rest, as they say, is history.

Fortune favors the bold, and some of us need to take bold action. If we are assessing our life and find it wanting, now is the time to make the decision to follow our dreams.

Setting Goals

Achieving your ultimate goal means setting smaller, daily goals. Keep them attainable, and make sure they are in line with your ultimate goal. Maybe you want to begin looking for a more fulfilling job—a position that aligns more closely with your why and with your ultimate goal in life. So your first small goal is simply to spend one hour updating that resume. Then tomorrow the goal might be to update your LinkedIn profile. The next day, to send out resumes to five companies that are potential fits based on your criteria.

Little goals, small steps, lead to bigger opportunities and changes in your lifestyle. This is why it is so important to take action—any action so long as it is in alignment with your ultimate goal. If your goal is to be the top salesperson in your group, take the small step to connect with five more potential clients that day. DM on Instagram, connect on LinkedIn,

Facebook, e-mail, and phone. Set a goal of a certain number of connections per day, and watch your sales increase.

Our goals will grow and evolve as we reach them, and each step we take leads to more opportunities and more decisions that we must make. Make those decisions with your why and your ultimate goal as guideposts. Many times this will narrow your path while other times the path will seem wider with many more side roads. Be careful that you don't start down too many different roads without following them to their end.

Follow One Path at a Time

With the internet and modern technology, there are so many available options and paths to choose for careers and businesses. Sometimes that makes it easy for us to begin many different things before being distracted or pulled down another avenue. Think about your current situation.

Are you saying things that you're going to do, but don't actually do them? What unfinished projects are on your backburner? What plans have you made but not yet executed? Why not? What exactly is holding you back? What great ideas do you have that you have not taken action on yet?

This is an important part of your life assessment. It can show you what is important to you. For some of us, we may find that these unfinished projects are important, but somehow we can't find the time to get to them. We might have hit an obstacle in our progress, and we've allowed this to stall us indefinitely.

For others, it's our daily habits that are keeping us from following through. How much time do you spend surfing the internet or watching television at night? How do you spend your time most weeknights? What about on the weekend? What about in the morning? Do you get up just in time to get ready and go to work? What's your morning routine like? Could you get up a little earlier to buy yourself some time to work toward your goal?

A big factor in finding the success you imagine is being honest about your failures, habits, and current situation. If you've read through this chapter and thought about these questions and now feel discouraged because you're not where you want to be, or you've got some habits that are holding you back, don't despair. It is never too late to try again.

And if you don't know the answers to the questions of why you're doing what you're doing and what your ultimate goal is in life, maybe the next chapter will be helpful. We'll go down this road a bit further as we explore the idea of being self-aware.

———

CHAPTER TWO

SELF-AWARENESS

*"Know Thyself" was written
over the portal of the antique world.
Over the portal of the new world,
"Be Thyself" shall be written.*

—OSCAR WILDE

"Just be yourself." Have you ever heard this line and wondered exactly what it means? "Just be yourself." Is it a command? A piece of encouragement? Am I not always just being myself? How can I be anyone other than myself? How do I act when I'm just being myself? Some say you are only your true self when you're completely alone.

And of course, we don't always act the same way *all* the time. Most of us don't talk to our mother the same way we talk to our friends, and when we're around our children, we don't act the same way as we do around our colleagues at work or in business. Or do we?

It can be a frustrating and nebulous ideal, but there are some things we can clear up as we move forward with exploring the concept of self-awareness. The idea of "being yourself" suggests that we should be comfortable in our own skin and not feel as though we should act in a way that is unnatural to our self. What else is contained in the idea of being ourselves?

When you know who you are, you have more control over your life, which gives way to a feeling of freedom no matter what walk of life you are in or how much money you have.

We are talking about knowing your strengths, weaknesses, and how you appear to and interact with others. It's not an overnight process to learn these things about yourself, but when you sink into who you are, it's a game-changer. It makes it easier to be positive; it makes you fear death less (and consequently other more mundane fears like discomfort) because you are comfortable with your life as you're living it, and this makes it easy to do the persistent work necessary to succeed. In short, when you know who you are, you become more productive and mindful of the present.

The present is where you are fully conscious and living from that space outside of all your problems, the ideas you have about yourself and your past. Living in the here and now, you get more done. You don't waste time thinking about what you should do; once you know what it is, you do it. In the doing of it, you lose the sense of anything outside the moment—for the most part. This is the value of the present moment.

When you don't know who you are, life is more of an act than usual. We all must act on the stage of life sometimes, but when you are unable to grasp the characters you are playing; it is more of a struggle.

Some people are lucky enough to know who they are and what they want in life from an early age. This usually stems from exceptional parenting. An emphasis on independence and self-esteem and an exposure to a variety of world perspectives and experiences in childhood often translates into confidence and authenticity in adulthood. But if you're not one of those lucky few, you can still come to know yourself no matter what your age or stage in life.

Self-awareness comes through effort and the gradual process of time, and if you are open to the truth, you will find it. You can become self-assured and achieve all that you wish to achieve.

You will know when you are on the right track because you will begin to find peace about decisions you make and activities you undertake. A big part of this is taking action, making decisions, and carefully observing the results. I will share many different ways in which observation and introspection are vital and can help you, but this process will also require action and lots of it.

You have to try different things to find out what you like and don't like. Introspection will take you part of the way—it can give you the right mind-set and will always be part of the process—but action is the game. Learn to take chances, and embrace the process of discovering who you are and the work that you love to do.

So how do you get to know yourself?

Write It Down

The art of writing is the art
of discovering what you believe.
—GUSTAVE FLAUBERT

One way to begin to figure yourself out is to write down your thoughts. Journaling. It's a simple, age-old process that is a fantastic way to get perspective on what is going on inside your head. If you're already doing this—good, do it some more. Some wait until the end of the day; I encourage you to do this throughout the day if possible.

Keep a small notebook with you and make a note when you think of a good idea. When you read or hear a good quote, write it down as soon as possible. Write about when you're embarrassed, angry, sad, motivated, or excited. You are looking to make a manifestation of yourself. This will be visible evidence of your thoughts, reactions, and motivations that you will be able to evaluate frequently. As it builds, you will have weeks, months, and years of your own thoughts to examine from a different perspective in time. A side benefit is writing in your journal during a meeting looks like you are furiously taking down notes from the boss.

Record Yourself

If you don't like to write, record your words and thoughts in another manner. With smartphones you can record audio or video easily, and there are apps that will allow your voice recording to be transcribed into a PDF. You can buy small, high-quality audio recorders that work as well—the important thing is to document your thoughts in some way on a daily basis. Do this especially when you feel emotional about something: whether angry on the way home from work, depressed on the way in, motivated after a good day, or looking forward to the weekend. Whatever it is, document those thoughts. Write them down, record them as you drive, or make a video if you prefer.

You don't have to show them to anyone but yourself, and it's a great way to start seeing how you respond in day to day incidents. You'll see your strengths and weaknesses, inclinations and inhibitions, what motivates and excites you, and what de-motivates you and causes you to procrastinate. Then you can learn and grow from this information.

When you get a collection of data—real-time data, day-to-day stuff—over a period of time, you will be able to recognize certain aspects about yourself and then accept or change them. If you feel silly doing these things, it's OK—do them anyway. Try not to think about it. Get used to yourself and the way you talk, look, write, and express yourself. The data you collect will go a long way toward figuring out who you are and what you value.

Your journey can change your life for the better in major ways, but you must first choose to embark on that journey. You must make tough decisions, and you must get past the discomfort of wanting to quit trying during those inevitable days when things seem less clear than ever. You have to start somewhere. Paying close attention to the thoughts that continually run through your mind is a great place to begin compiling information.

Straight Talk with the People Who Know You Best

Another way to get information about yourself is to ask others. This is a great time-saver too. We are not in a hurry—this is a lifetime journey—but it is important to reach a level of self-awareness that allows you to continue taking steps on your path toward your success. There should be a sense of urgency—not haste—about making progress.

Successful entrepreneur Gary Vaynerchuk offers the suggestion of creating a collaborative self-assessment event with the five people that are closest to you. It might be your spouse, a sibling, a friend from work, a parent, and your college roommate. It might be a strange mix of people, but you get them together for a couple hours and ask them to tell you what you are good at and what you are not so good at. It's an uncomfortable step but an extremely useful one when it comes to figuring out who you are and what you want to do.

A less confrontational way to do this would be to simply send out e-mails to these people asking for responses to those questions. The problem often is that most people don't want to be honest with those they love when it comes to subject matter like this. It's important to find out the negative as well as the positive, and if you are able to ask these questions, it provides useful information toward knowing who you are, what you are good at, and what you're lousy at.

If you are fortunate enough to know people who care about you and who will be honest about their full perspective of you, take advantage of this. It can save you a lot of time, but it has to be coming from people whose perspective you value and trust.

When I was preparing to go back to college, I used this exercise to find out about myself, but also to find a specific direction to take and one that has served me well, many years later. People enjoy being consulted and trusted to offer this sort of feedback. Not everyone responded, of course. But of those that did, there were several responses that suggested the same or similar paths to take in choosing a major, a career to study in college.

Not all advice given was specific. Some of it was philosophical, and some responses were filled with the lessons learned the hard way from many years of experience. The main takeaway for me was—and this came mostly from people who were older than me— if you can help it, make the money side of your choice secondary. Meaning, don't pursue a career just because it pays well.

For me, I was looking at what to study to earn a degree and give me a chance at a fulfilling career. With all that I knew about myself, I wanted to pursue English. Many people said that is was a useless major, a degree with no prospects of earning money unless you were to use it to get into law school or eventually get your doctorate. In any case, I took the advice of those who recommended not using the potential earning power as the guide. I don't regret it for a second and this simple exercise was instrumental in helping me get into a line of work that complemented my strengths and interests—my unique DNA.

It's important to remember that becoming self-aware is a gradual process, not necessarily a place or state at which one finally arrives. There are varying degrees of self-awareness, but it is essentially a way of life more than a point of achievement. These exercises and ways of seeing yourself from other perspectives are building the foundation for the improved version of yourself.

Let Go of Your Past

Similar to finding your goal and finding your why, we have to recognize the things that get in the way of self-awareness, and one of those roadblocks is the pain of the past. Many were hurt in their childhood, in adolescence, or in relationships later in life, and they carry the pain of that hurt with them into their present and future. They live with that pain, and that pain feeds on other people's pain. It becomes impossible to discover who you are and what you should be doing when you are blinded by your pain and the pain of others. That's why it is sometimes necessary to distance yourself from people—even members of your own family—who carry around pain that they refuse to put down.

If you are carrying around the pain of your past, you simply will not be open enough to receive information about yourself. Your focus will be elsewhere, and you will be defensive and dismissive toward what you learn.

It reminds me of a guy I used to work with years ago. He was in his late twenties or early thirties during the time I knew him and possessed an impressive memory and way of seeing the world. He was the type of guy that could recall the names of obscure actresses from movies seen one time ten years ago. The perspective he would bring to conversations was always original, and he shared his opinions with a sharp wit and sense of humor.

But he was self-deprecating to a fault, constantly talking negatively about himself and his circumstances. He self-medicated with pot and beer and considered his job at the warehouse a necessary evil and a good job for someone like himself, a highschool dropout. Inside, he was an angry person. His mom abandoned him as a young child and his father was a drunk. He moved in with a friend in his early teens, eventually dropping out of school, getting a couple of DUIs and some jail time. But the worst thing was, he could not see a way out. As an outsider, I could only list the ways for someone as intelligent as he clearly was to be able to change his situation. But he couldn't hear me. He didn't believe it. He was told growing up that he was a loser, a mistake, and he carried those labels and the pain with him.

Many of us get everything right except for this part of releasing our pain. It becomes an obstacle that prevents breakthrough. After time, it is natural for people to develop an unhealthy affinity for their pain and sadness. It's a ready-made excuse to stay exactly where they are.

In childhood, we develop defense systems—some might call them shells—to shield ourselves from the cruelty or difficulty of life. Imagine the true self hiding beneath that shell. The shell or the shield blinds us to who we might be. Some of us need to come out from the shell, put it down, and face life as it is instead of dwelling on what we remember it to be.

Many of us are holding onto our parents' mistakes. We are still judging them for their failures and blaming them for ours, but our failure is ours to own because we have a choice now. We have a choice about how we are going to live and how we are going to react to the circumstances we find ourselves in today.

I would encourage you to look around you, recognize and be thankful for all the good in your life now, and stop using your past as an excuse for your current dissatisfaction. You can't overestimate the power of gratitude to help change your perspective. Constantly choose gratitude. Burn it in your mind; it will be the spark of light that begins to overpower the pain of your past.

Choosing gratitude means being thankful for the world and your opportunities within it rather than wishing for the good old days. As we live out of a state of gratitude, we start recognizing chances for success and ways to achieve our goals using the tools that are at our fingertips. Sometimes, these tools and chances are the ones we were too busy complaining about to notice the potential benefit they carried.

Bad Habits

You will be as big as your dominant aspiration,
small as your dominating desire…
—JAMES ALLEN

As the British philosopher James Allen points out, your ultimate goal can easily be missed in favor of an overriding addiction or habit. On a micro-level, as we're talking about being self-aware, habits can slow this process or stop it entirely in many different ways, but the most notable is that they are a welcome distraction from the mundane. We need to be present in the mundane because by paying attention during those times of boredom and the typical, we find the hidden truth about ourselves.

There are increasing numbers of people who spend inordinate amounts of time on the internet because it is a distraction that is available 24/7 nearly anywhere you are with a phone. It's so easy to stay distracted in today's world; it takes a level of discipline to turn devices off and just think, write, record, or be present in the moment, but it is essential. Pay attention to when you lose time without anything to show for it. For example, if a chunk of time has gone down the tubes, and you experience no concrete benefit—such as an awesome time with your family, planned downtime for yourself, or work that you've put in toward your goal—it's worth noting that what you were doing during that time might be a bad habit.

Something Good Now or Something Better Later

How many people believe they are the better version of themselves with substance use? It could be a drink to make us more social or a pill to relax the nerves and make us a better listener or planner. Maybe it's medicine that helps us be more attentive and alert.

It can be easy to ignore the side effects of these substances. Before we know it, our tolerance is up, and a little bit becomes a little more and a little more. We delude ourselves when we think we are more productive, creative, or interesting under the influence of drugs. Sometimes it takes getting this idea out of our head and participating in life without these crutches to realize that we can be better without them.

Keep trying. Fail and try again. Don't accept your addiction or habit as part of yourself. It doesn't define you. When I was trying to quit smoking after years of a pack-a-day habit, it was a challenge just to go into a convenience store to get coffee and not buy cigarettes. Many, many times I failed. But some days

I succeeded and would go without smoking. I looked at it as a small victory—one less day of the harmful effects of smoking—and I kept on trying to quit. Then I would go two or three days before I failed again. Then a week, a month, before I finally quit for good.

We have to gain control of our impulses in order to gain control of our life. It doesn't mean we won't make mistakes, but we can't let them get the best of us. If we are wasting money and time on our addictions, then we are losing money and time that could be going toward our dream.

To reach your goals, you have to decide between something good now and something better later. Keep that goal first and foremost in your mind when you are tempted by a bad habit. Record your thoughts about it, and notice what triggers the urge to indulge.

Social Awareness

Social awareness is different than caring too much about what others think. It is more about understanding how you appear to others, how you interact with them, and how your words and actions cause them to feel. I'm not talking about every single interaction, but in a general sense, do you know how you are perceived by those around you on a consistent basis? Or do you only *think* you know?

You can use the following as a rough template for e-mailing questions to close friends and family members that may help you learn more about yourself. Adjust the language as you see fit:

Dear Friend,

I am on a journey of self-exploration in order to better fulfill my purpose in life. Would you please give your honest feedback to the following questions? Please don't avoid answers that are critical of me in this assessment. The negative parts of me may be the most important information for me to learn, and I will hold no ill-will toward you for your answers. Thank you for your help.

What are the positive attributes or character traits you see in me?

What are the negative character traits or behaviors you notice in me?

What do you see as my skills in a professional or career sense?

What do you see as my weaknesses professionally?

What do you wish I knew about myself that perhaps I don't?

If you were me, in what area of interest or career would you invest your time?

Thanks again for your candid answers,

Your name here.

The next step is to act upon what you are learning about yourself through all this collected and recorded data—this concentrated effort to get to know yourself and how you appear to others. From this material, you can learn exactly what your values are, what your strengths are, what your weaknesses are, what your goal is, and what your motivations are. You can learn how much of what you consider "you" is truly you and how much of it is made up of ideas about yourself that you've accepted and carried over the years as if they were true. Then you act on this knowledge. You begin putting in the work you know you need to put in.

Synchronicity and Flow State

When you act on what you've learned about yourself, you begin to start acting as an authentic individual. It makes you aware in a way that you weren't before, and you'll begin noticing increased instances of synchronicity—in fact, you'll notice more in general because you've started paying attention to little details you never had time to observe before. Synchronicity is a concept introduced and explored by the psychologist Carl Jung, and it is the phenomenon/idea of coincidental occurrences having meaning due to the lack of a causal relationship.

For example, my son and I were talking one night about robots and the hypothesis of the uncanny valley (the idea that a humanoid object that closely, but not exactly, resembles a human creates eerie feelings and a sense of revulsion in us). My son had read about it in an article on the internet earlier in the week, and it was the first time I had heard of the concept. The *next day* when I came home from work, my son held up a magazine that had come in the mail that day and featured an article on the uncanny valley. Synchronicity. Jung used it to explain his ideas about the paranormal; I see it at least as evidence of the energy that lies outside of human explanation. When you are living in a more self-aware state, you will notice frequent occurrences of this nature. Use them as indicators that you are living closely in alignment with that code of DNA that is uniquely yours.

When you are living from this space, ideas will come to mind with a clarity you've never experienced before. You will start falling into stretches of what is known as the flow state. The flow state is when you become one with who you were meant to be and what you were meant to be doing, and you are fully immersed in the present moment of activity. Time becomes less concrete and less crushing and more like the construct that it is because you are living in the present and doing what you want to do—what you were meant to do. When you start experiencing this, you'll find the motivation to do more of it.

Authenticity and the Ego

Authenticity results in more productivity because you care a little less about what other people think of you. You stop falling prey to the wiles of the ego. See, the ego is what you think about yourself; it is the ideas you have about what others think of you; it is what makes you experience yourself as "I." So when you say, "I like to eat chocolate," this is your ego. The daily activities of the day are managed by the ego. It's a necessary part of our makeup, but it has some negative side effects. The ego is what causes the curse of self-importance, which tells you that you should be offended by somebody's actions or insulted by words spoken to you or about you. It makes you take things too seriously and prevents you from letting go of that which you cannot control.

The more we give attention or preference to the ego, the more distance we put between ourselves and our true purpose/calling/DNA. While it allows us to build an identity, the ego also separates us from others—it creates the illusion of separation—and when we get outside the ego, we can see how over-identification with it becomes an obstacle on our journey to personal success. When we identify too closely with the ego, we begin to believe we are the things we own or achieve, what others think of us (our reputation), or the way our body looks; we begin to identify as a body separate from everyone else and the energy of the universe. All this subconsciously leads us to believe we cannot connect with our true self nor live the life we desire to live.

Are you your name? Or were you given your name? You were given your name of course, just as you were given other information which helps to make up the ego. Again, the ego is a necessary part of our existence, but life gets out of balance for us when we decide that we ARE our name or reputation. This is where disconnect comes in: we can't hear our inner voice—the part of us that existed before our name and exists outside of our ego.

We only become what we are
by the radical and deep-seated refusal
of that which others have made of us.
——JEAN-PAUL SARTRE

When you become grounded in who you are, you take action that is congruent with your foundation, and you no longer live by praise or criticism. You live by reality. You live according to what is instead of what you wish was.

While the ego can never die, as you live more authentically, you rely less on its importance—meaning, you stop taking your "self" (the ego-driven construction of the mind) so seriously. You recognize your ability and freedom to give words power—or to choose not to. You begin to allow yourself to embrace paradoxes.

Embrace Paradoxes

From a universal perspective, nothing you do is of grand importance. Recognizing and accepting this will give you the freedom to imagine that the most tedious efforts are worthy of great care and attention. This paradoxical idea has the ability to introduce much higher quality to the work you do. It allows us to off-load stress by embracing the absurd notion that no matter how important we think our problems are, the universe will keep floating on, completely indifferent to our worry.

Paradox lets you believe you are awesome while also recognizing how inconsequential you are. It allows you to care about what others think while also not really caring at all. Paradox is embodied by that person who is incredibly competitive while somehow one of the most cooperative people you know. These are examples of contradictory ideas/characteristics existing in the same space, and it is essential to accept paradoxical ideas when coming to acceptance of certain aspects about yourself and others.

The idea of embracing paradoxes will be an important part of this journey. It is when you truly realize that you are nobody that you are free to be anybody. So who are you or who are you going to be?

Focus on Your Strengths

The mind is constantly being filled and refilled with new thoughts and ideas, but stick to what you learn about yourself, double down on your strengths, and try to minimize your weaknesses, and you'll realize your dream/goal. Everybody has weaknesses, so don't let that slow you down; pay attention to and build on your strengths.

Once you realize your strengths and weaknesses and accept this information, embrace what you've discovered, and take immediate action. This might mean quitting a job, starting a business, or changing careers. Whatever you find out about yourself, it's not enough to know it; you have to take the next step. You have to act on the things you learn.

Here's the thing: no one can tell you what your next step should be. Only you can, and you have to take it. Maybe you know what the next step is because it scares you or it bores you. It is the thing that you must overcome to find the satisfaction, energy, and passion that you seek in life.

Take the step you've been putting off for years due to fear or due to a lack of belief in your own abilities and intuition. You are armed with confidence and the knowledge of who you are, what you like and do not like, and most importantly, what your goal of success is in this life, however you define success.

Some of us need to take action before anything else can change.

One more thing to remember is that this life, this hustle, this ambition, this self-awareness, and this social awareness is never finished. It doesn't end until we fade from consciousness one final time. Otherwise, life is different moments, days, years, events, people, and the play goes on. We are not looking for an ending to work our way back from, instead we are finding a new perspective that allows us to continue setting and reaching goals.

Awareness is the way. In the end, we are playing a part, a role. Remember Shakespeare's words: "All the world's a stage, and all the men and women merely players: they have their exits and their entrances; and one man in his time plays many parts..." We must become aware of this fact physically and emotionally rather than just intellectually. It is then that we will see that first brick come loose in the wall, and once we see through the opening to the light on the other side, we must overcome our fears and keep taking the action necessary to break through.

———

CHAPTER THREE

NO PARKING IN FEAR

Courage is the price
that life exacts for granting peace.
—AMELIA EARHART

Following a life assessment and an exploration of the self, you may find that you've learned quite a bit about yourself in a short period of time. You may have discovered not only what you are good at but also what you love to do. Perhaps you've realized that you need to do some work in the social awareness department. Maybe you've come to realize that big changes need to be made in order for you to bring your daily life into alignment with your life goal.

In many cases, this is the point at which people tend to get stuck and not move on because they identify with a fear or they are hesitant because of a fear. They know what needs to be done, but they stay parked in fear, time passes them by, regret builds up, and they never know who they could have become and the things they could have accomplished.

Fear is fine. It is what triggers our survival response and what has allowed us to evolve into the race and civilization we have become, but when we let it dictate our actions without real cause, we lose. Most of our fear is imagined consequences, anxiety about events which have not and likely will not happen.

Act in the Face of Fear

There are of course many things in modern-day life that scare us—some of them legitimately—and there is no way to get rid of the emotion of fear, but there are ways to overcome it. To act in the face of fear reduces its impact on our lives. This is the concept you must own and hold close as you continue on your journey toward empowerment and success.

When the actress Charlize Theron was 15 years old, her alcoholic father came home in a drunken rage, firing his shotgun at the gate of the house. He continued to fire his gun and yell and threaten Charlize and her mother before eventually crashing inside and firing into the kitchen where they were. Thankfully, her mother managed to get her handgun and shoot him dead before he killed them. Though Charlize rarely speaks of the event, she offers this brief insight into how she became successful despite her intense childhood distress:

"It was the great tragedy of my life, I think what follows is…you have to find where you want yourself to be, and how you want people to see you in this world. I had a parent who led me through the grief, shock and anger going through all of the emotional things that you do when you—when something like this happens to you, …[and it] really kind of guided me towards not being a victim and not going through my life feeling victimized." (*Charlize Theron's Childhood Home Scene of Grisly 2012 Murder*)

Charlize Theron overcame the lasting effects of witnessing this horrible event through her mother's guidance, but also through her own decision to act when she could have held onto the fear, sadness, and trauma of this situation. It could have caused her to put her life in park, but instead she decided who she wanted to be and what she wanted to do, and today, she continues to live the life she chose.

There is always a choice to act no matter how scared you are, and this is the beginning of overcoming any singular fear. One way that fear gets the best of us is we surrender our mind to dwelling on the negative results that could come of the action we are about to take. In our inherent desire to live risk-averse, we over-estimate the bad consequences while downplaying or ignoring the possible benefits of our action, and it is nothing more than a mental game.

If we play up the positive and continually remind ourselves of the goal we are after and our reason for persevering, we will take the action and find the reward worth the fear. After repeatedly doing this in various circumstances, a funny thing starts to happen: we become a little less fearful in general. We become less hesitant about making decisions, and perhaps most importantly, we start seeing the world in a more positive light. We start to see the positive side of people and judge them a little bit less because we recognize that most negativity from others comes from a place of pain and fear in their own life.

I believe that most fear has at its root the fear of death. For example, fears of insects, spiders, snakes, and germs all have been established out of the risk they posed to our life in primitive times. They still pose a risk, but not to the same extent as we are more educated about the risks and have built safe, sanitary habitations, have advanced medicine to treat bites, symptoms, sicknesses, etc. In the same way, I believe phobias like the fear of public speaking, social anxiety, and talking to strangers are left over from the fear of being ostracized from society for not following social norms and thus not being able to find food and shelter to live. Fear is the instinct that allowed us to live and evolve. But the risk of dying outside of natural causes is much lower today.

Though of course we will die someday, think about the ways to overcome this fear as well. It's been said that the things we do for ourselves, we take with us when we die, but the things we do for others, we leave behind. That's the way to create a personal legacy that lives on after your death. Use this idea as motivation to do more, create more, and be more valuable and helpful to others so that your memory lives on by the way you've touched the lives of those who remain.

Facing the Fear of Criticism

Many of us stay parked due to a fear of criticism, but the more you become self-aware, the less you will be affected by the criticism of others. There is always a crab-in-the-bucket mentality among humans that makes us want to pull the one back who is trying to escape the lifestyle of the rest. It's easy to criticize the person who stands up and stands out, vulnerable to the crowd in an effort to become who they want to be instead of who society says they should be.

Fear of criticism can be overcome by recognizing and owning who you are, your good points and your flaws, and secondly, by recognizing your place in relation to the society you live in and the characteristics and inclinations of that society. Many of us are born into a system that encourages competition over creativity. If we have little to no competitive nature, we would be better situated in a different time or society, but we have to recognize where we are and how we fit. There is a way to find your place and your people and a path to your successful life.

This is an important societal truth. Another is that not everyone will like you. It doesn't matter why; it is just an indisputable fact of life that some people will like you and others will not like you—with or without justification.

When children are not taught this important fact— if they are not taught that their self-worth is not dependent on other people's approval of them— they become what is often called people-pleasers or approval-junkies. This parental mistake could lead them to do everything and anything to please other people because that's where they find their value, and it makes them especially susceptible to the fear of criticism because, instead of being able to shrug it off for what it is, they take it as a personal attack on the core of who they are.

Hear criticism, shake it off, and forget it if it's not constructive. Maybe it's something you need to hear, something you didn't know about yourself. If this is the case, try to learn and grow from it. Other times, when you're becoming someone who takes action, someone who creates culture, people may try to discredit you. They may try to pull you down and say negative things about you behind your back, but pay them no mind.

When you are constantly wrapped up in your racing thoughts about what others think, you are actually unaware of yourself and the way you truly appear. When you reach a level of self-actualization that allows you to see yourself as you truly are, you might have some repair work to do among friends and family, but this is a healing step in the right direction. Generally, we think people care much more than they do. This creates a personal need to put forth an image, to pay too much attention to how we appear to others. The truth is that others just don't care, and when they do, it's usually not for the reasons we would think or want.

Be aware of your motives for acting and speaking. Don't get involved in speculation. Don't do anything just to be liked or thought well of. Do things because they are right things to do. Say things because they are right things to say or because you believe them.

Getting over the Fear of Failure

What if I start my business, it fails, and I lose all my invested money and time? What if it fails and I lose *other people's* invested money and time? What if I take this other job and it turns out to be worse than my current one? What if I try sales and I turn out to be lousy at it and don't make enough money?

Again, fear is founded on looking too much at the downside and not enough at the upside. If you quit your job to start a business, the loss is very clear—your current source of income—while the gain may not yet be quantifiable or visible. It takes mental focus to try to estimate the upside as much as the downside. For example, a person who wants to make this step—quitting a job they hate—but is scared because of the lack of income, misses out entirely on the potential income lost because of the way loathing your job creates mental blocks and muddiness. It can't be shown on paper, but the relief, clarity, and uplifted mind and spirit brought on by leaving a negative situation is of incredible value.

And failure can be spun into a positive thing as well, if you think about it. A guy who is always starting businesses and failing or always inventing new devices that never quite work, this guy, at the end of the day, will be remembered for his efforts. He'll be remembered by his loved ones as a guy who never quit trying, and who knows, maybe one day one of his businesses will take off and become successful. The point is he isn't defined by his failures; he's defined by his perspective and his lifestyle.

In fact, if you are not failing at something at least once in a while, you may be parked in fear. You're not doing anything if you're not trying and failing, and it takes that failure to learn, do better, and grow with the next effort, which all increases your chances of success. Failure is to be embraced, not feared.

Michael Jordan, arguably the best basketball player ever to play the game, said this about embracing failure: "I've missed more than 9000 shots in my career. I've lost almost 300 games. 26 times, I've been trusted to take the game-winning shot and missed. I've failed over and over and over again in my life. And that is why I succeed."

It's the trying, failing, and trying again that eventually gets you on the path to success.

For some, it's not the failure itself that scares them; it's the consequences of that failure. Specifically, they fear the loss of income.

Releasing the Fear of Poverty

The fear of poverty is often associated with the fear of failure, but it is one that can be overcome by believing in yourself and having a firm grasp of your values. I'll never forget one of the lessons I learned about the fear of not having enough money while working in a machine shop in my twenties.

There was a guy who was in his sixties who worked near me on second shift, and we would often talk over lunch break and throughout the night. He was a guy who had worked in many different places and shops and had all kinds of stories from each one. One night, he told me the story about starting a job at a machine shop years ago and how, on his second day, he saw the owner of the shop come out on the floor and blow up on one of the other machinists, cursing, swearing, and being verbally abusive. He said, "When I saw the way the owner treated that guy, I packed up my toolbox, told the supervisor I was quitting, went out to my truck, and drove home." He had three young children, a wife, a house, and not much money in the bank. He explained, "I came looking for a job, and I'll leave looking for one, but I won't work for someone who treats other people that way. There's no job worth giving up your self-respect for."

At the time I knew the man, he was nearing retirement, and his children were grown and had completed college, two were married, and they were all in successful careers. I guess they had learned quite a bit from their father's actions. He maintained his character above money or job security, empowering himself and his family to live with integrity and peace instead of regret and shame.

That story always stuck with me because I knew that a guy like him would never go without a job for long because he was confident in who he was and what was important to him. I also realized that there was a good chance that the man who had endured the abuse that day went home, grumbled to his wife, and returned to work the next day. The difference between the two was the fear of poverty.

It is never too late to release this fear and believe in and respect yourself enough to know that you will survive no matter what. You will not go hungry, and you will sleep well at night knowing you can choose your circumstances without the fear of poverty clouding your judgment and eating away at your self-respect. Choose to release this weight.

In his book, *The Power of Intention*, Wayne Dyer looks at times when he left stable positions because he had to follow his heart. Here is his story about one such instance:

"When I left a professorship at a major university for writing and public speaking, it wasn't a risk; it was something I had to do because I knew that I couldn't feel happy with myself if I didn't follow my heart. The universe handled the details, because I was feeling love for what I was doing, and consequently, I was living my truth. By teaching love, that very same love guided me to my purpose, and the financial remuneration flowed to me with that same energy of love. I couldn't see how it would work out, but I followed an inner knowing and never regretted it."

Follow your heart. Are your actions motivated by love or fear?

Accept Confrontation

Do you hate confrontation? Do you do everything to avoid confrontation?

Sometimes, confrontation is key in gaining self-respect and confidence. Regardless of whether the confrontation is a little thing or a big thing, the ability to confront another individual, the ability to express your feelings about something negative or offensive, is crucial to understanding who you are.

If you constantly bury your feelings and words within yourself in order to preserve other peoples' feelings, you are suppressing yourself, and you are lying to yourself and others about your life. You're in constant disagreement with yourself. It's not authentic behavior. Just by nature of being human, you will offend and be offended. To pretend that this is not the case, or to pretend not to care when someone hurts you, is to deny your humanity and deny your worth as a human. That other person is not worth more than you, so why would you think that their feelings should be preserved from offense at the expense of your own?

It doesn't make sense except within the framework of inauthenticity, façades, and self-loathing. President Harry Truman said, "We must have strong minds, ready to accept facts as they are." The more we ignore truth and circumstances, the further into ourselves and our delusions we withdraw.

Confrontation, then, is an essential part of our humanity. If we suppress it out of fear, we've lost something of what makes us *us*, and we've given into fear which hurts our social confidence.

Sometimes, there are things you have to say regardless of the consequences. I mean things that, if you did not say them, you would be doing yourself and others a disservice. It's likely that these things are uncomfortable to say or address. Address them. Say them anyway. Do it with as much grace and tact as possible, and let the chips fall where they may.

When I worked on a construction crew years ago, I remember the five of us loading up the truck one Monday morning around 4 A.M. The foreman on the crew was an intimidating character—I'll call him Willie. He was the kind of guy who barked when he bothered to talk at all, no regards for accepted manners of polite society—a tobacco-chewing, cigar-smoking, whiskey-drinking fellow who seemed to be perpetually disgruntled. That was Willie.

On this particular morning, there was a new guy on the crew, his first day. As we were getting supplies around, Willie yelled at him, "Hey! Grab that spool of wire and throw it on the truck!"

The new guy, Ron, was missing one of his two front teeth and half of the other one. Later, he would proudly tell me the story of how he lost them thirty years earlier as a twelve-year-old fighting a sixteen-year-old. His arms were marked by jailhouse tattoos and his face with scars of various shapes and sizes.

When Willie yelled at him, Ron didn't hesitate to respond.

"Whoa!" he said, "We need to get something straight right now. My name is Ron and I wouldn't let my own father talk to me that way. You understand?" Willie understood, called him by his name, and spoke to him with more care from then on. Ron set his boundaries in this case.

Other times, you have to learn not to confront and cause issues when time or other circumstances will take care of it without your involvement. If you have to let someone know they crossed a line with you, handle it and let it go. Let them know your boundaries, but you have to rise above it in the end. Deal with it and then rise above it. If you let it consume your mind and your best energy, then you are wasting valuable moments, and you have only yourself to blame. Don't keep rehashing it. Avoid paralysis by analysis. Get to work.

Sometimes confrontation goes well; other times people aren't receptive to it. Find another angle if necessary, but confrontation can be and is healthy if it's handled in a professional manner. Remember too that confrontation in a relationship does not equal dissatisfaction, and being honest and staying present-focused helps to overcome negative sentiment.

Approval-Seeking Behavior

I've realized throughout my life that a good number of us who struggle with fear of confrontation are also approval junkies. It makes sense. When you go through life trying to meet the impossible task of making everyone like you, inevitably you fail. You wonder why, and you wonder what you did, and you wonder what that person thinks and this person thinks and what that person said to this person about you. You become scared to say or do anything that someone else might not like or that might make them not like you.

Do you like everyone you encounter? Why would you expect others to just naturally like you?

Much of the approval-seeking behavior comes from growing up in environments where we weren't taught that it is OK to be yourself. We weren't taught that it is OK if not everyone likes you, that there are so many different kinds of human beings in the world. That it is OK if you don't like everyone or get along with everyone and that it is also OK if others do not like you. Not everyone will like you, and it doesn't have to be for any legitimate reason; what people deem as legitimate varies anyway. The world keeps turning regardless of what you think of others or what others think of you.

Some of us grew up believing our happiness is dependent upon others being pleased with us.

We needed to impress other people. We needed to make them smile, make them laugh, make them compliment us in order to feel self-worth. Unfortunately, just the opposite was happening. We were giving our self-worth away.

In order to get out of your parking space of fear and move forward, know and believe in yourself and your values, and live without the need for the approval of others!

They're All Gonna Laugh at You!
Overcoming Fear of Rejection and Ridicule

What is the fear of rejection when examined? Is it the fear of pain? The fear of being alone, stemming from our tribal roots? It's not a physical pain we're afraid of. It is emotional and mental pain, and therefore, it is controllable. It is able to be monitored, and it really isn't the big deal we imagine it to be. From an early age, rejection stung: your parents not playing with you because they had more important things to do, your friend sitting beside someone else in school because they were new friends, your peers picking you last in the playground games, and the girl or boy you had a crush on laughing at you. All of these painful experiences contributed to a layer of conditioning that taught us to fear this pain.

Rejection—being laughed at, shut down during a sales pitch, turned down by a potential suitor—becomes more manageable the more often one experiences it. So one solution to overcoming the fear of rejection is to intentionally put yourself in situations where you might be rejected or ridiculed. The more it happens, the less you'll care, which is not a negative reaction but a natural one. Open yourself to rejection, and you will realize that it doesn't matter too much. Once you realize this, you'll move past its power.

When you are rejected in circumstances similar to the ones mentioned above, what happens? Your feelings get hurt—sometimes a little, sometimes a lot. You might be embarrassed. What else? Not too much.

We blow up the consequences of rejection to such an unrealistic level in our minds that we allow our imagination to dictate reality. Accordingly, we avoid these "catastrophic" social situations where we're likely to be judged.

Go to that party, apply for that sales position, ask that girl or guy out, and make that phone call. It's not that big of a deal. Fear, embarrassment, and pain are part of being human. They are extremely typical human conditions and emotions. You are not unique in your experience of any of them.

Get uncomfortable in order to see things from a new perspective. Outside your comfort zone is growth. If you're scared, do it—unless you're scared of bungee jumping or sky-diving. Your fears may be well-founded in those cases.

Here's a mental exercise to try that can help you picture the idea of letting go of the fears you hold onto. It's called "Six Months to Live."

Six Months to Live

Imagine.

Imagine you are healthy and in the same circumstances as you currently are except that you are driving home from an appointment with the doctor at which you learned that you have a rare, incurable disease that will bring certain death in no more than six months. You and the doctor are the only two people who know, but it is an unquestionable truth. You will not necessarily go through a painful sickness; you just know that on the last day of six months, you will not wake up.

Driving home, you are lost in the deepest thoughts and emotions you have ever experienced. Everything is more vivid, more real, but less serious. There's a numb but pleasant feeling that courses through your body as you drive. Then you think about what you'll tell your loved ones, and when.

You instinctively feel that each meal, each hug, each handshake will take on new meaning. There is no feeling of dread at your impending death, but instead, you fully embrace the freedom that this knowledge brings. You worry much less about making deadlines and getting things done that need to be done—incidentally discovering that it is easier to get things done. You stop worrying about others' thoughts of you. You find yourself no longer procrastinating or hesitating to do things unless you are sure you want to procrastinate. Then you do.

You make the phone calls and the connections you had been wanting to make but hadn't yet. Human relationships become important to you like never before. New friendships blossom.

You stop caring about what people think of how you are living or what you are creating, selling, or writing. You find that you have more than enough ideas and time. You feel sad about the idea of leaving your loved ones, so you spend more time with them whenever possible. Now, there is no time for remorse, no time for regret or feeling sorry. The time goes by fast, and you care deeply about leaving something of significance, something of worth to humanity.

Would you die regret-free in your current lifestyle? Are you living your dream or are you living your fear?

If you can relate to any of these different kinds of fears we've discussed in this chapter, I encourage you not to give up, and don't let yourself be defined by them. If you get anxiety about talking to people, force yourself at your own pace and in your own way to move through that fear. Now, it should be noted that not every fear you have must be overcome; we're talking about fears that prevent you from living the successful life you envision. That may not require getting over a fear of spiders, but it may require getting over a fear of public speaking or talking with others.

Keep your goal in front of you and foremost in your mind, and put yourself out there—you never know what will happen, but you know for sure what will happen if you stay put, frozen in fear. Go after your dreams. Ask for that raise or promotion by being confident in your abilities. Whether you are looking to start your own business, expand a hobby into a business, or succeed in a particular field, don't let your fears be a roadblock to your success. The more that you face and overcome those fears, the brighter the future becomes, and it is far easier to have a positive outlook on life knowing that it is not so serious and daunting as you might have imagined.

———

CHAPTER FOUR

CHOOSE POSITIVITY

Change your thoughts and you change your world.
— NORMAN VINCENT PEALE

Jim Stovall was a big, strong athlete in his late teens with a promising football career ahead of him. When the doctor diagnosed him, he was told that he would eventually lose his eyesight entirely. The news was crushing, but Jim still worked hard on his athletic endeavors; he became an Olympic powerlifter and played football into college as long as he could before his vision became too poor. Then one morning at the age of 29, Jim lost his eyesight completely. He was blind. In his book, *The Art of Optimism*, Stovall describes that day:

"I rushed into the bathroom, turned on the light, and stared at where I knew the mirror was hanging over the sink, but there was, quite simply, nothing there. The dreaded diagnosis had become reality, and I began the adjustment of learning to live my life as a blind person. I was 29 years old, I had never met a blind person, and I did not have a clue what I was going to do with the rest of my life." (p. 20)

For a while, Jim did struggle with emotions, with not wanting to leave his nine-by-twelve-foot room in his house, with the negative attitude that he could have chosen for the rest of his life. No one would have blamed him. There was nothing fair about the circumstances he found himself in, but that's not what Jim chose. After a little old lady who lived down the street gave him a cassette tape recording of a talk by Dr. Denis Waitley, Jim Stovall played the tape, listened to the material, and decided to choose positivity.

To date, Jim has written forty books and seven of them have been turned into movies. He writes a weekly syndicated column, "Winner's Wisdom," and founded and runs a television network (*Narrative Television*

Network) which provides television and movies for blind people. He speaks to millions of people in arenas worldwide, spreading hope and optimism and giving incredible advice to anyone who chooses to pay attention and use it to change their life for the better.

It's easy to think positive, be positive, stay positive, and talk positive when life is going well for you. The fork in the road—when you are faced with trials, with pain, with circumstances in your life that may be outside of your control—this is when you have a choice. When there are plenty of negative aspects to the situation, and you can easily choose to focus on them and feel angry or sad, or you can look for and focus on the positive aspects—that's your test. You can find the opportunity in the challenge, the silver lining of a bad situation or tough circumstances.

For the purposes of this chapter, we can look at finding positivity and optimism through two avenues: Attitude and Action. These are two keys to break through many obstacles in this journey to personal success. Let's look at how we can adjust our attitude to create positive energy.

Find Gratitude

What's good about today? What am I excited about? What do I have to be thankful for today? We live during an amazing time of opportunity and technological advancement—look at what you have, look at your lifestyle, look at your relationships, look at all the chances you've been given, and find a perspective of gratitude. The fact that you were conceived at all is against incredible odds. Were you born in a country where you are free to choose your occupation, your religion or lack thereof, your partner, and your living conditions?

When you start being thankful, it's hard to be negative, and when you start choosing to look at life from a perspective of gratitude on a consistent basis, you will find that it is much easier to do so. When negative things happen—not necessarily catastrophic, but little things like losing your keys, spilling a drink, having a flat tire, getting into a fender bender, etc.— you'll find yourself staying calm instead of cursing or getting upset in the way that maybe you typically would have in a similar situation in the past.

Note yourself thinking poorly and stop yourself.

Self-fulfilling Prophecy

The way we think dictates how our life turns out. If we think in a negative way, more negativity comes into our lives. If we choose to think positive thoughts, more positivity is attracted into our lives. This has been proven as fact over the years. This is why it is so important to control the mind, choose your perspective, and weed out negativity from your life. This can be followed to the most micro of levels, including the absentminded small talk in which we sometimes engage with others.

Watch the words you say. "It's been a long day." "I feel like crap." "Tomorrow's going to be rough." Statements like this seem thoughtless and normal, but they create negative thoughts in our mind. Pay attention to the words that you say without thinking because there is thinking involved whether you realize it or not. Once you say the words, or immediately before you say them, they are in your mind and you give them thought. Choose positive statements or none at all when given a choice.

It is important to live life with a certain awareness of yourself and others so that you notice when conversations in which you are involved start to take a turn toward negativity or complaining. When you notice this, try to change the conversation into a more positive one or politely remove yourself from the encounter.

Negativity, like positivity, spreads fairly easy. Unlike positivity, negativity causes people to feel empty, sad, and fearful, which causes them to reach for crutches like shopping, alcohol, food, or other substances that help them temporarily to feel more complete and safe. It is a huge tactic of the media and corporate powers to spread negativity to control consumer behavior. Choosing to spread positivity and goodwill is the beginning of improvement in societal relations.

Now let's look at choosing positivity through action.

Create Your Own Culture

We have to create culture, don't watch TV, don't read magazines, don't even listen to NPR. Create your own roadshow. The nexus of space and time where you are now is the most immediate sector of your universe, and if you're worrying about Michael Jackson or Bill Clinton or somebody else, then you are disempowered, you're giving it all away to icons, icons which are maintained by an electronic media so that you want to dress like X or have lips like Y.—TERRENCE McKENNA

Sometimes negativity doesn't come solely as a result of the news, politics, or internet content but in the form of attitudes and energy from other humans. There are all kinds of negative energies that can surround people in any family, office, factory, warehouse, car dealership, church, or any other communal space. Notice and gravitate toward optimistic people in a social situation, and make it a point to hang around people who have positive attitudes about life.

You and your family (your partner, children, friends) can create your own traditions; don't just consume what society tells you to consume. Don't do anything just because you're supposed to or because that is how it has always been.

Have boundaries when reading, watching, or listening to the news. Ask yourself how it might be affecting you. Depending on the channel you're watching, America is devolving into totalitarianism or fascism and the imminent destruction of civilization as we know it, and it's all the fault of the other political party, identity group, activists, etc. The constant bombardment of stories about natural disasters, mass shootings, terrorism, political corruption, and scandal is not good for anyone's mind. Raising awareness and funds to help those affected is one thing, but consuming this sensationalistic tragedy as entertainment through social media feeds or a television that is always tuned in to the news could affect your attitude in negative ways. For some, it aggravates nerves and actually raises blood pressure.

Violence, tragedy, and controversy sold newspapers years ago, and it sells views, advertisements, and a spirit of fear today. Try to avoid it. You'll have plenty of problems of your own, so try to keep your entertainment and reading material positive.

Look for the Helpers

The late Fred Rogers, better known as Mr. Rogers from the PBS show *Mr. Rogers' Neighborhood*, offers another perspective of how to handle the news through a childhood memory:

"I was spared from any great disasters when I was little, but there was plenty of news of them in newspapers and on the radio, and there were graphic images of them in newsreels.

"For me, as for all children, the world could have come to seem a scary place to live. But I felt secure with my parents, and they let me know that we were safely together whenever I showed concern about accounts of alarming events in the world.

"There was something else my mother did that I've always remembered: 'Always look for the helpers,' she'd tell me. 'There's always someone who is trying to help.' I did, and I came to see that the world is full of doctors and nurses, police and firemen, volunteers, neighbors and friends who are ready to jump in to help when things go wrong." (*The Mister Rogers Parenting Book*)

We see what we want to see. Mr. Rogers reminds us that we can decide to see the good in life, and that even in the worst catastrophes, there is something positive going on.

Of course this doesn't mean that we should avoid all discussion of news, politics, philosophy, etc., but we should be selective with whom we talk about topics like these. Have these conversations with individuals who welcome healthy debate and people from whom you might learn something through an argument on different sides of an issue.

Don't hold onto your opinions so tightly that you lose rationality and decency when your views are questioned. Remember that they are ideas, just thoughts and beliefs that you have adopted due to your upbringing, education, and life experiences—nothing worth getting upset about.

Live your beliefs and ideals in your own life; treat people with kindness. That's how positive change will happen, not through calling each other names on YouTube comments. It's been said many times, "Your beliefs don't make you a better person, your behavior does."

The Internet and Social Media

We are all now connected by the internet,
like neurons in a giant brain.
—STEPHEN HAWKING

Because we are all connected by the internet, it is easier for ideas to spread further and more rapidly than it once was. We must be aware of this and choose to consume and spread positive rather than negative information.

We walk around with the combined knowledge of the world in our pockets and at our fingertips—the smartphone. With the constant connection to ideas and information, there is a danger of people forgetting how to think for themselves and choose the information they consume rather than have it fed to them through social media. There's no need to introduce jealousy, negativity, and phoniness into your life via your smartphone. There's plenty of that already. I encourage you to put the phone away for a while, turn off the social media, and watch your problems diminish.

Make it a point to talk to people wherever you are. At the gas station, the grocery store, say hello and make small talk. Challenge yourself to make some kind of connection. When you are feeling depressed about not being productive or about anything else, talk to someone. Grab the phone again, and call a friend or a family member who would appreciate it. You may be surprised by how much better you feel afterward.

Get Involved with Community

Another way to let go of negative thoughts and choose positivity is to find a way to get involved with the community. Find out how you can visit people in the hospital or nursing homes—people who have it much worse than you and who could really benefit from a simple visit from another person. You could volunteer time with the homeless shelter, an animal shelter; you can volunteer your time as a tutor or help out at the local public library. There are numerous organizations with which you can volunteer and gain the benefit of feeling better while also helping others to feel better. Be a blood or marrow donor.

The more we look outside of ourselves during rough times, the better we will feel. Look for opportunities to help others and keep your mind off your troubles.

Find Opportunity in Problems

When you are able to start putting an optimistic spin on negative circumstances, you have the ability to do the same with your day-to-day problems at work and in your relationships, viewing them as part of your goal. Problems become opportunities.

Opportunities bring the potential for reward and growth. Instead of shying away from problems, you can look forward to finding the good in them to see where it leads or what could be improved. There are often opportunities for improvement in the little problems that we notice recurring in life. That's why it pays to be aware and notice the patterns of events, actions, and reactions in your daily life.

All of life might come down to this idea of choosing and changing your perspective. The power of this ability means that nothing is as definite as it seems and that we have incredible freedom at our fingertips. We have the freedom to choose the way we see life, the way we see the world and its mysteries, happiness, and heartbreak. What a gift!

Are you thankful for your relationships, material comforts, and experiences? If you knew you would die today, how would your thoughts be characterized? By disappointment or gratitude?

There is so much good in our life today! Look around, read a paragraph or two from a book, see the beauty in nature, go for a walk, go for a drive. Dissatisfaction often arises from not staying in the present moment. Learn to accept the present moment as it is—without wishing for changes, more possessions, or situations to be different. There's a difference between working hard for goals and staying in the moment, and wishing for things in your mind, daydreaming, fantasizing, without being in the moment where you could potentially do something useful toward achieving your desires.

It can be an ongoing battle to bring yourself back to gratitude and back to the present moment. Doing this is the key to not letting one or two negative occurrences ruin your day and derail you from focusing on your goal. Find the goodness; it's all around you.

Focus on what you have, not what you don't. You might argue that this contradicts the whole point of reaching for and achieving goals, but I don't think so. When you focus on what you have and live out of a state of gratitude, it allows you to be a more optimistic person, which motivates you to do more, to take more action, and brings you closer to your goal. Conversely, if you focus on what you don't have and live and work from a place of want, you'll find negativity and frustration due to the inner belief that you don't have enough.

Don't cry because it's over, smile because it happened.
—DR. SEUSS

Patience and Awareness

Another way to bring positive energy into your life
is to wait out the negative feelings. That's right, good
old-fashioned patience. Our emotions are often
cyclical. When you are feeling low and sad, give yourself permission to feel this way, knowing that you will
soon feel much better. This advice is not for when you
are sad or depressed about something specific like the
loss of a loved one, but for days when you wake up
with a general sense of melancholy or ennui that you
can't seem to shake and that has no real source you
can name. Be OK with it and let it pass.

Alternatively, when you're feeling low, angry, or sad—
think "stop," and forcibly change your thoughts to
ones you enjoy. Think about or do whatever calms
your mind. Within this frame of thinking, you can
find peace and quiet from the noise and the negativity. Today, focus on the good things in your life.
Color your glasses with gratitude. Pay close attention

to how your emotions change with the thoughts you choose.

The more aware you become, the easier it is to control the mind and be positive. You'll be able to accept times when you feel sad and depressed and know, through experience, that you will be happy and positive once again before long. You learn to ride it out.

It's become cliché, but only because it is so true. If you want to achieve a measure of success in life, no matter how you measure it, a positive attitude will be necessary to achieve your goal. Anyone can give a number of reasons why one shouldn't have a positive outlook, but the same person could give a number of reasons why one should. And at the end of the day, why not?

There will be challenges, heartbreaks, and deep losses throughout life. We know this to be true. We have to decide right now, before we face what is to come, how we are going to react to these incidents. It is often said that we are in control of our thoughts and should be able to think positively or negatively at will. This is not entirely true. We are able to choose how we react to the thoughts that come into our mind, but we are not always in control of what thoughts enter in the first place.

It's OK to feel negativity. We all feel low and depressed at some point. It's important to remember that we are not all born equal with regards to the chemicals in our brains that cause contentment and sadness. Sometimes prescribed medication is necessary for individuals who are predisposed to depression because of their chemical makeup.

In any case, it is important to control what we can about ourselves. Many times it is as simple as putting a positive spin on our situation no matter how far-fetched that positivity might seem. Positivity breeds positivity. You have to start somewhere even in the most dire of situations.

Positivity comes in different forms. Some people laugh and smile; some simply act in a calm, practical manner. If it is bringing peace and improvement to your world and the world in general, it is a positive action.

"Fake it till you make it." This is an often repeated phrase in the personal development world. It works sometimes. Try smiling when you don't feel like smiling. Try laughing when you don't feel like it; laugh out loud. Positivity can be called forth through action.

Take a walk. Do some push-ups, sit-ups, or jumping jacks. Physical activity can lead to emotional activity. Motion creates emotion. Get up and do something if you are feeling low so that you regain positivity and focus on your goal.

Positivity through Exercise

Not only does exercise boost your mood, but you can really get to know yourself through exercise. It oxygenates the brain and gets the creative juices rolling. It also gives you time alone.

Exercise aids brain power and offers surplus energy. It boosts chemically enhanced feelings of positivity and pleasantness while burning unnecessary fat and building healthy muscle.

And it is of utmost importance in reaching our goal of self-awareness and our goal of personal success. Why? It keeps us healthy. Maintain your health to keep a good quality of life. We can also exercise to replace bad habits that prohibit us from reaching our goal.

Pick an activity that resonates with you. Hiking, swimming, yoga, and martial arts training are some good activities filled with physical exercise. But it is important to find something that you enjoy to some extent. Then do more of it. You will find that it begins to rise on your list of priorities after several weeks of making a conscious effort to include it in your schedule. You will even start looking forward to it. Now keep the habit going and live a better life. One of the beautiful things about exercise is that it begins to influence you to be a more productive person. It causes you to think more clearly about your goal; it incites ideas and action to help you achieve personal success.

The exercise habit begins to attack procrastination. Those are just some of the benefits of working out regularly.

Maybe you're not sure where to start when it comes to exercise. Start by taking a walk. Then take a walk the next day and the day after until you are taking a walk each day. The benefits of simply walking each day will be enough to motivate you onward. After that you might move onto the running, bicycling, swimming, yoga, weightlifting, etc.

Walking for a while at night or in the morning—anytime really—is helpful to let the mind exercise itself with the body. The mind and body make connections during physical activity, and that physical activity allows the mind to rest and the body to stay healthy. It's a reciprocal effect. It's important to exercise and view exercise as a remedy and an outlet during, after, or before times of stress and anxiety.

Staying Positive through Stress

Our brain manufactures scenarios for us to feel stress about that usually do not come to pass. As a result, we become focused on solutions to problems that only exist in our mind. Understanding this can help us calm down quickly.

Meeting deadlines, attending meetings, and maintaining budgets produces stressful thoughts in many of us. Relationship issues, car issues, and parenting issues trigger stress in others. What is it that stresses you out the most? Write it down.

Can you control any aspect of it? Maybe you are worried about what you are going to wear to work for the big presentation on Monday. Take the time to pick out your outfit down to the smallest detail, and make sure everything is ironed and ready a day or two in advance. If you are worried about what you are going to say and how, rehearse your presentation in front of others, and record it on video so you can review it.

Having a nightly routine can be helpful in beating stress. Some ideas for activities to make a part of your presleep routine: meditating; praying; reading; watching; or listening to motivational, humorous, and/or inspirational content. Evaluate your day, and determine what you did that brought you closer to your goal and what distracted you.

Staying Positive in Negative Environments

It's unlikely that you'll be able to be a positive person in a negative environment without a clear exit strategy, complete with a deadline, or without some other clear, truthful, and self-agreed *why*. If there is one thing I emphasize, it's this: do not waste years at places you don't wish to be. I know every day isn't the best day no matter where you work or what you do for a living, but I'm talking about working at a place or in a career where you constantly complain and give off negative energy—and again, this might be something you don't recognize about yourself. This goes for churches, jobs, clubs, whatever.

If you don't like it or don't agree with the philosophy of management or the mission of the church, leave. The door still opens both ways. Get out as soon as possible because not only are you hurting yourself with self-conflicting behavior, you are making it harder on the people who do want to be there or are working on a positive strategy to do something else. You're not just wasting time; you're wasting health and mental ability.

All that said, if you are comfortable and honest about your reasons for being in this environment (and for you younger readers, it may be your parents' home), you can still be a positive person in a negative place surrounded by negative people. Maintain your values and your work ethic at all costs, and do not let the environment dictate who you are. Set goals and give yourself a timeline. If your goal is a certain amount of money, make that amount clear and reachable within a set amount of time, and work hard to accumulate it.

Just remember, there are many ways to earn money, and there are many people who would be happy to employ you if you have the desire and ability to learn and work hard. Bottom line, in a negative environment, maintain a strong sense of self, and work hard to get out of that situation. If your principles—your non-negotiables—are being compromised by working there, it's time to go. Never stay in a position with a company at the cost of your self-respect.

If you don't have something going as a side project, get it going by deciding what it will be today. It's not only useful as a plan B if you lose your current job, but it is useful in that our time is limited but possible experiences and skills are not. To learn a new skill or try your hand at another business on the side is a way to take advantage of these possibilities. Whether you want to learn to play an instrument or learn a new trade, get it going in the hours before and after your regular job. This goes for whether you like your job or not.

It will bring you relief and newfound interest. When things are rough in one area of your life and you need to shift focus, it gives you another goal. Hobbies are useful in this way, but don't let them be enough to keep you in a place of dissatisfaction when it comes to work. There are too many opportunities out there to remain in a place that creates feelings of strong negativity within you. Again, the damage and lost opportunities can't be put on paper, but they are every bit as real as your salary.

Have a plan and stay positive.

To close this chapter, I want to share some encouraging and challenging words from Christian Larson (1866–1955) in a piece called "The Optimist's Creed."

The Optimist's Creed by Christian Larson

Promise Yourself

To be so strong that nothing can disturb your peace of mind.

To talk health, happiness, and prosperity to every person you meet.

To make all your friends feel that there is something worthwhile in them.

To look at the sunny side of everything and make your optimism come true.

To think only of the best, to work only for the best and to expect only the best.

To be just as enthusiastic about the success of others as you are about your own.

To forget the mistakes of the past and press on to the greater achievements of the future.

To wear a cheerful expression at all times and give a smile to every living creature you meet.

To give so much time to improving yourself that you have no time to criticize others.

To be too large for worry, too noble for anger, too strong for fear, and too happy to permit the presence of trouble.

To think well of yourself and to proclaim this fact to the world, not in loud word, but in great deeds.

To live in the faith that the whole world is on your side, so long as you are true to the best that is in you.

People who choose optimism can be comfortable and confident in themselves. This means they know their strengths and weaknesses, they accept these features, and they live on with gratitude for the experience. Does this mean they're always upbeat and positive? No, life is made of ups and downs, highs and lows, and mostly the in-between, but you can always choose positivity and choose to focus on your strengths and be grateful. Make choices each moment.

Change what you can. Accept what you can't.

If you think positive thoughts about yourself, others are more likely to do the same. It's true that it doesn't matter what they think—and you can't always guess their thoughts anyway—but you'll give off positive energy, and people will react in kind. Your problems are mostly a result of negative self-talk. Turn that inner voice around to speak positively about yourself and others, and you'll soon start being more optimistic and more comfortable around other people.

It is hard to overemphasize the importance of being positive on your journey to personal success. Your choice of attitude really can make or break this process, and it will be critical to maintain an outlook of optimism as you face all kinds of different obstacles along your way.

I encourage you to choose positivity when faced with a choice, and every day we *are* faced with a choice. Some days the positive outlook is easier to choose than other days, but we want to get to the point where we are choosing the positive outlook every day, every morning when we wake up. Each day we can ask ourselves: what attitude/perspective will I choose today?

What can I do to add value to the people and the culture around me?

When you choose positivity, it makes it easier to stay in the present moment and be able to make good decisions about what to do next. Stay positive and stay present—your successful life awaits!

CHAPTER FIVE

STAY PRESENT

Be not the slave of your own past.
—RALPH WALDO EMERSON

Throughout life, there is a temptation that often plagues us. It is the desire to look back on pain or pleasure or to look ahead at challenges. Both choices come at the cost of the present moment, and we sacrifice productivity, concentration, and creativity when we let our minds wander.

Try not to look back to the past and recall painful memories. Move forward toward personal success by keeping your thoughts squarely on the present moment, and remember not to dwell too long on accomplishments either. Stay present to create value in the current moment, and enjoy your life right now.

By staying present, you can work harder for longer periods of time. When you start drifting off into speculation, worry, or fantasy, remind yourself to come back to the present moment—the here and now—and get back into what you were doing. Control your thoughts. Don't wonder about responses to e-mails or texts that you sent; don't let your mind wander to *what if* questions. There really is no *what if* or *if only*; there is only today and this moment. Be here.

This level of concentration and conscious effort will allow you to reach your dreams by consistently bringing your attention back to the work that needs to be done. As you get practice in doing this—redirecting your thoughts in this manner—you might find yourself enjoying a deeper sense of contentment and satisfaction in what you are doing at that present moment. It won't be long before you get into the flow state and lose track of time, and that's when you know you're doing the right thing. It starts with being aware in the present moment.

We often lose our attention to the present right after something negative or stressful happens—or any interruption, really. Do you need to take that phone call? Do you need to make that appointment right this second? When you're involved in a project, try to stay with it as long as you can without interruption.

Letting Go and Moving Forward

When you write or speak with regularity, you will eventually write or say something stupid or make an embarrassing mistake. Dismiss the resulting feelings as quickly as possible, and come back to the present moment. Make amends where needed, but don't prolong painful, embarrassing, or anger-filled circumstances by thinking or talking about them for too long. Let them go.

Consider the following lines from Ralph Waldo Emerson about closing each day and starting a new one; his words capture the power of now.

Write it on your heart

that every day is the best day in the year.

He is rich who owns the day, and no one owns the day

who allows it to be invaded with fret and anxiety.

Finish every day and be done with it.

You have done what you could.

Some blunders and absurdities, no doubt crept in.

Forget them as soon as you can, tomorrow is a new day;

begin it well and serenely, with too high a spirit

to be cumbered with your old nonsense.

This new day is too dear,

with its hopes and invitations,

to waste a moment on the yesterdays.

—Ralph Waldo Emerson,
Collected Poems and Translations

Start each day fresh and appreciate the gift of the present.

Try not to waste time thinking of the things you should've said or could've done differently. How many times do we replay the events that upset us? What about exchanges between us and another person in which we (or our ego) felt insulted by the things they said, but we didn't say anything or didn't know what to say at the time? After we've thought about it for hours and talked about it with our friend or spouse, *now* we know what we *should have* said.

Maybe we put our foot in our mouth with a knee-jerk reaction, and now we are filled with regret, wishing it hadn't happened or that we could go back and change our actions. Maybe we overanalyze others' actions and words and ask ourselves questions like: Why did they say that, or why don't they like me?

So much time is wasted with thoughts like these. So much creativity is wasted in the time spent mulling over conversations that are long over, words that linger only in the mind. And as another side effect, our awareness is deadened.

When we sit and ponder what might have been, we give up our power to create, our power to be aware, and our power to overcome the past. We give up what we might gain in exchange for going back to a past event in our mind that has already been changed by our thoughts. So we take what is now compromised (our recollections of this past event) and give up what's real and true (this present moment). It's not a smart trade.

What is it that happens when we let our minds wander off into thoughts of anger, shame, regret, or resentment? We waste the present—the only time we truly have.

It can be challenging to maintain attention to the present moment, but there are different ways to regain it when you lose it. Depending on the circumstances and what you are unconsciously choosing to entertain, the following tactics can be used to concentrate the mind and come back to reality.

Accept and release the thoughts that disturb you. Accept and release—this is one of those paradoxical ideas. The idea is to release thoughts rather than resist them so that they pass through your mind and disappear. I'm talking about thoughts that hurt your feelings, thoughts that bruise your ego and damage your perception of yourself—sit with them and allow them to float through your mind…and then let them go.

Dwelling on past hurts and negativity is yet another form of procrastination. It's not personal—your ego is looking for an excuse to be offended and thus to feel important. The truth is your feelings get hurt because there are other people in the world. Conflict is life, life is conflict, and it is many other things as well. Live and act from empathy.

It feels good to vent to a partner or a friend about the things that hurt and offend us. At times it might be necessary to sort out the details of an issue in order to gain proper perspective and move forward appropriately. If this is the case, have this conversation after your work is done, or talk about it and let it go so that you can refocus and stay present. But remember, there's no need to talk about every negative word you say or that is said about you or to you because sometimes it only serves to give those words and feelings more power.

A key to happiness is staying in the present moment. Staying present, doing work you enjoy, having fun, facing life's challenges and responsibilities. It is the stuff of life. It's contentment, and it comes from having inner calmness. After our basic needs are met, contentment comes from within. Let the heaviness pass away, enjoy the good times, feel the sadness and sorrow during the bad times and know those feelings are temporary.

Coming Back to the Present through Sensation

Another technique for gaining control of your attention and bringing it back to this moment is to take note of physical sensations. If you are sitting in a chair, place your hands on the arms of the chair and feel it, notice your feet flat on the floor; if you are walking, feel each step you take and look at your surroundings. The key is to give greater attention to the smallest details of what you are physically doing. That is why it is helpful to concentrate on your breathing.

A friend of mine taught me a technique he called "red roots." Envision bright red roots growing from your feet deep into the ground. These roots are strong and keep you grounded. Every time you feel yourself losing control, whether in nervousness, annoyance, impatience, or any other unwelcome emotion, you find your red roots. It's as simple as saying "red roots" to yourself and then imagining, really picturing, those roots growing downward from your feet, through your shoes, through the floor, deep into the ground.

When you do this, you are forced back to the now, back to what is, and it gives your mind the opportunity to reboot and focus on whatever you want it to focus on, rather than wandering through the catalog of thoughts and memories and fantasies and questions that you have stored or that happen to pop up.

Concentration

In influencing others; just as in
mastering yourself, the true test of efficiency,
the secret of success, lies in the ability
to concentrate the attention.
—NAPOLEON HILL

A key to concentration is learning how to cut out distraction. What distracts? Why does it distract? Why do we let it distract us? Are we looking for an excuse to procrastinate? Are we scared of failing with our work? Do we simply not want to do what we are doing? Maybe we're unsure of how to proceed, so we allow ourselves to be distracted?

Keep focused on one thing at a time. The ability to concentrate is your biggest asset.

Constantly checking e-mail or social media is a costly addiction. Choose times when you don't answer or check e-mail. Choose times when you do. Close it. Your phone can be a constant distraction—welcome or otherwise—as well. Make it a point to work without them if needed, but if they are needed, use them, but don't let them use you.

E-mail and your phone can be extremely efficient tools, but when used improperly, they can be real productivity killers. Master the art of concentrating the attention. It's a task that comes much more naturally as you practice your techniques of coming back to the present moment and refocusing.

Time Management

Time doesn't exist, clocks exist.
—ANONYMOUS

There is no time. There is not enough time. If only I had more time.

How often have you heard these lines? Many times, probably. One of the above statements is true, however, and that is, "there is no time." Time is an idea. It's an exceptionally valuable human invention of the abstract. We use time to test inventions, medical procedures, and security systems. We use time to track progress and evolution and to plan important events and meetings. We use it to create ages and calendars—we use time all the time.

But time is not a substance like water or dirt. Why can time be bought and sold? Why is one person's time worth more than another's? Is it possible to "buy more time," and why is there such a focus on time management?

Here are some principles to consider in understanding these concepts and questions: each moment is all we have, and this is true for everyone. Our brain power has allowed us to create the concept of time and use it to our advantage. We can decide nearly every moment how we are going to spend it. Even when we are working or doing something we would rather not do, we can use that moment, that time, for our benefit.

When a person decides upon a desire or a goal for her life, she will use more of her moments to focus on and work toward her goal. When she succeeds, she will be consulted by others and asked, "How did you achieve this?" She will explain how she used her time. Now her time becomes more valuable. She increases its value within the universe by not only achieving her own goals but also by helping another person achieve theirs.

Time is our collective description of all of these individual moments. The moment right now, as you are reading this line, passes by as quickly as you read or hear each word, right? Now it has become part of "time."

It is essential to your success that you understand that time is an idea and that it does not need to carry the crushing pressure that it often does. Break it down into moments. Keep focused on the present one while keeping your goal in the back of your mind.

If your goal is to have a certain number of dollars by a certain age, then question yourself the moment you get ready to hand over money for a fast-food sandwich or a soda or something trivial that you could do without. By staying aware in the present moment, you are buying time. Each of these moments adds up to your time. So if you deny yourself the soda, you not only saved money toward your goal; you just added to the time you spent working toward that goal.

Time management can get complicated, but keep it simple. Focus on your goal and stay present in each moment. There is no past, only present. Prepare for a potential future, but now is all that is. Present-forward is the mind-set to keep you going.

What's in a moment? Everything. It's all in the moment. Now is forever. What will you do with it? Put this mental spin on the weight of time, and you will see your stress decrease and your productivity increase.

Managing Expectations

When we imagine conversations and engagements that we are looking forward to, there is a temptation to either overestimate the positive aspects or overestimate the negative aspects of the encounter or event. When you go to a meeting, a sales call, or any similar event, try to pay attention to your own internal goal without projecting expectations onto others. Stay focused on the present moment and how it aligns with the goal that you picture in your mind—your overall big picture, burning desire goal—and go on without further expectations.

You cannot control people, and of course you cannot control the outcome of chance events, encounters, nor other happenings in the universe. The best way to manage the anticipation of success or failure is to manage your expectations. Try not to expect. Try to be and do. Let the chips fall where they may, but be true to yourself and your goal.

Don't fall into the trap of expecting people to see you as you see yourself. Learn to follow your instinct and your personal truth without relying on actions or reactions of other people. The mind is better open to experiences than filled with thoughts of the future. Too much time spent in the future means missing out on the present. Experience. Don't expect.

Stay focused on your goal even while entertaining ideas from others. I am amazed by how easily and profoundly I am affected by a certain book, movie, or speech. That's the power of words and ideas and a big reason that I love publishing and the written word—it's an opportunity to share and trade ideas and start conversations. Remember to maintain a focus on what needs to be done because, in addition to all their good qualities, words and ideas can be distracting. They can create unrealistic expectations and sway you from your goal.

Reducing Stress through Physical Awareness

Pay close attention to your body the next time you feel stress within you. Name the source of that stress. Feel your chest get tight, the blood rise, and any other physical sensations of stress. Breathe deeply. If possible, move away from what is stressing you, and move toward an activity that can bring you closer to your goal or will make you laugh.

By following these techniques over time, you will reduce your level of stress. You can learn to take things less seriously and enjoy life more. You can stay out of conversations that you know will bring you stress, and you can begin to decline invitations to events that bring more stress than benefit. This is progress.

Eventually, you will start spinning your perspective on circumstances rather than just accepting your initial reaction. This is the way to calmness in stressful situations. You begin seeing things for what they are on a macro level rather than whatever story is being made up in your mind; that's when you can begin controlling the story or shutting it down altogether.

When you're calm in mind and spirit, problems don't bother you as much—thoughts don't keep eating at you like they used to. Your time—moment by moment—continues to pass; what you are at the end of that time is, in part, the result of the choices you made in handling stress.

Look at the Beauty and Goodness of Life

Driving my car one day, I had a thought, and a lingering sensation accompanied it. It was a dose of the profoundly temporary nature of life—I experienced the reality that I could be in an accident and die that day. I felt peace and existential bliss, and it gave way to a perspective that helps me to keep the senseless notions of self-importance ever in the background.

When I begin to dwell on thoughts of workplace stress, financial worries, and relationship fears, I laugh, step back, look around me at all the beauty and silliness and goodness, and think, "I'm alive and here is life, and I'll enjoy it while I'm here."

Let your experience inform your reaction to stressors. You know it will turn out OK. You know the negative feelings will pass and be replaced by positive feelings—or at least neutral feelings. So you might as well take everything with a grain of salt, as they say. Stay calm. Everything will be OK.

It starts with you. When you find calmness within yourself, you will feel it in your reactions to other people, situations, and stress—no matter if it is social stress, family stress, relationship stress, financial stress, or emotional stress. You'll be able to keep your heart rate down and feel life in all of your body parts and extremities. You will feel calm, peaceful, and present with what you are doing or with whom you are interacting.

One more tip is to appreciate the immediate circumstances in which you find yourself living.

Live Fully Where You Are Now

Much of our discontent comes from not fully engaging with and appreciating our current situation. I encourage you to enjoy the town or city you live in. Get to know the people. Instead of worrying about the problems of the nation and world, find a way to provide value to your local community in some way. Find a way to start being more involved in the job or occupation you find yourself in. How many of our problems would fade if we would change our perspective enough to lessen our thoughts about what we want and what we don't have and focus on the *now*? To adjust our view of the present in this way will allow us to really focus and do the work necessary to change the aspects of our situations that we wish to change while allowing us to find greater fulfillment and contentment where we never would have imagined it: the place where we are right now.

As you conclude this chapter, consider these words from Epictetus (a Greek stoic philosopher who lived from A.D. 55–135):

Caretake this moment.

Immerse yourself in its particulars.

Respond to this person, this challenge, this deed.

Quit the evasions.

Stop giving yourself needless trouble.

*It is time to really live; to fully inhabit the situation you
    happen to be in now.*

You are not some disinterested bystander.

Exert yourself.

Respect your partnership with providence.

*Ask yourself often, How may I perform this particular
    deed*

*such that it would be consistent with and acceptable to
    the divine will?*

Heed the answer and get to work.

*When your doors are shut and your room is dark you
    are not alone.*

*The will of nature is within you as your natural genius
    is within.*

Listen to its importunings.

Follow its directives.

*As concerns the art of living, the material is your
    own life.*
No great thing is created suddenly.
There must be time.
Give your best and always be kind.

—Epictetus, from *The Art of Living*

These motivational words sum up this step in your journey and place importance on the next step: work.

CHAPTER SIX

EMBRACE THE PROCESS

We work to become, not to acquire.

—ELBERT HUBBARD

The process of achieving our goal is a long and rewarding one. It's a construction area for as far as we can see, and we can work, grow, and learn through it all. You'll know that you're doing the right thing when you're looking forward to doing it most days. I'm not talking about a forced cheerfulness; I'm talking about a genuine feeling of inspiration and satisfaction that comes from the enjoyment of doing quality work. This is when you'll start turning to your work as an escape instead of trying to escape your work. The struggle will change from dreading going to work to having to intentionally plan time away to avoid becoming a workaholic. And as you'll be living authentically, it will be easier to find this balance.

When you experience the creeping feeling of self-doubt or regret about decisions you've made or anxiety about something coming up, go put in work. Find something productive to do and start doing it. Do this repeatedly and you will discover a hidden power: the power to concentrate. This power increases your ability to control the mind, and once you learn to control the mind, there is little you won't be able to do.

Try this the next time you are feeling depressed: Think of something that you can do to be productive, and concentrate the mind on that single activity. If you are building something, feel the weight of the hammer, and watch as it connects with the head of the nail. Or the next time you are reading or watching a movie, concentrate on the words, meaning, and larger ideas of the material you are consuming. What are the pictures showing and implying? What can you learn from every situation you find yourself in?

It's a short step from this mind-set of forcibly concentrating the attention to an increased ability to remain focused on a consistent basis.

Put in Work

It is important to learn about your craft—research, attend seminars, read books, watch videos—and then to do the work based on what you have learned. Don't make the mistake of getting caught in the research and development phase of your goal. Make a list of steps that need to be completed to reach your goal, and begin working on those tasks and checking them off your list.

You can begin working before you are one hundred percent sure of what you are doing and how it will turn out. Learn as you work and work as you learn. Don't put off the action because you become too attached to an idea of expertise based on education and knowledge alone. Become a practitioner of your pursuit.

Take a couple minutes and consider these few questions:

What tasks are your priority today?

What will you do today to bring you closer to achieving your goal?

What have you already accomplished today?

What else is on your list?

Learn to love the process, immerse yourself in it, and push yourself. Work more.

Create, Don't Compete

Keep creating. Don't let the poison that is creeping into your mind destroy you. Don't compare yourself to others and get caught up in competition, working to prove someone wrong or to do better than someone else. Work hard for your goal in order to discover your purpose and to provide value. Pay attention to the people who are actually creating. Watch what they do. Ignore the naysayers and doubters.

Whatever your goal is, it is a creative endeavor. Your life is a creative endeavor as you consistently work to improve aspects of your situation or your health, and while there is a competitive nature to humanity, there is also a great spirit of cooperation. Along the way, you may meet others who are on a similar journey. There may be an opportunity to encourage each other and give feedback and support. Empower yourself and others through cooperation and joint efforts when possible, but otherwise focus on constructing your own reality.

When you focus on achieving your goals, you will find you are too busy to worry about what others think. This is a form of mental freedom that allows you to create the circumstances you desire, and as a by-product, you will be an example to others who wish to do the same.

Keep Showing Up

You have bad days, especially early on when you are learning something. When you first start riding a bike, playing a sport, or practicing an instrument, it can be frustrating. But if you keep coming back to it and keep trying, you will learn and grow competent in that skill or activity. Soon it will be second-nature and enjoyable to do the thing that was at first so difficult.

It's a truth that has been proven time and time again. If you want to learn persistence, keep showing up. It doesn't have to be a long road if you take it a day at a time.

Maybe when you think of persistence, you think of a runner running a marathon, or a mountain climber climbing Mount Everest. You imagine words like "long," "painful," and "time-consuming." Like many words, the word "persistence" only represents an idea. There's no need to get bogged down in the details and images of the word and what it represents to you.

If you want to learn how to do something, keep that goal in mind and continue to try day by day. If you want to start a business, keep working through one step at a time to make that happen.

So if you are engaged in a step or stage that is on the path to your goal, you are being persistent. When you stumble along that path or come to an obstacle, get back up and find a way over, under, around, or through that thing that is in the path. Persistence is action. Persistence is repetition. Persistence is focusing on the rung of the ladder you are on and then climbing up to the next one. It is not *always* action though. Sometimes persistence means thinking about a problem or a course of action for a long time before deciding to take action. Whatever the step, be engaged with it.

Work through Hard Times

It was early in the morning on October 31, 2003. Bethany Hamilton was on Tunnels Beach, Kauai, with her friend Alana and Alana's brother and dad.

They were looking forward to a beautiful day of surfing off the coast of the oldest of Hawaii's main islands. Bethany had lived and breathed surfing since she could remember—she was only eight years old when she entered and won her first surf competition.

On this October morning, having finished runner-up at the US National Championships earlier this year, Bethany's career seemed to be nothing but blue skies ahead. But Bethany's life would be forever changed in a few seconds time as she laid down on her board and paddled out to catch a wave.

It was 7:30 A.M. when the fourteen-foot tiger shark struck and attacked her. Her left arm was ripped from her body just below the shoulder, and her friends rushed to help. They managed to get her back to shore and use a surfboard leash for a tourniquet, and by the time she reached the hospital, she had lost sixty percent of her blood.

Bethany mustered her spirit and faith and would recover to full strength, but without her left arm. She was determined to return to surfing. It was just a month after the attack when she was back on the surfboard, and she continued to practice using customized boards and learning how to surf with only one arm. Hours upon hours, days upon days, she overcame emotion and put in the work of learning how to do what she loved again. After gaining competence, she continued to work until she returned to major competitions early in the next year, winning and placing in numerous events throughout the next years of her life.

There are always people who show the rest of us that fear and tough circumstances can be overcome if only you place your goal in front of you and continue working. Bethany Hamilton is one of those people, and her dedication, fearlessness, and hard work are characteristics to be emulated on your own personal success journey.

Go All In

Don't do it if you're not going to go all the way. If you're just going to half-ass it, don't do it at all. If you're only half in, then you're half out. You're lying to yourself. If you're going to do it, buckle up and get ready for the ride. Get ready for the pain. Use the pain; let the pain flow through you, swallow you up, and spit you out on the other side where you'll emerge a stronger version of yourself.

Don't make the mistake of dismissing a goal or an activity as too complicated when it is something that you want to do or achieve. Take it apart. Do one thing at a time and reach for your dreams. Remember, your whole existence is made up of these passing seconds. Make yours count. Put them toward something you want to experience rather than letting them float away unremembered and insignificant.

When you do what you don't want to do, it's never as uncomfortable as you imagined it would be. It's the doing, the getting started, that takes mental effort, and it's worth it. Do it. Start today. Don't wait for the time to be right. Go all in. The time is never right. The time is now, and now is forever.

It may be that the task you need to do to get started on your goal seems overwhelming, tedious, or complicated. Do it anyway. Put yourself into it one minute at a time; that's the way to own it and stick with it and not give in to the demons who threaten you with temptation and distraction at every turn.

Persistence. Make it happen today. Get through this day before you quit. You can quit tomorrow; just keep at it for one more day and see what happens. Feeling like death and dying? Push onward. Forward. Wanting to pass out and go to sleep? Give ten more minutes. When you feel like you've put in a long day, remember that someone out there is still working, still putting it in, still getting it done. Stay hungry. Do not give up, not yet, not tonight. Stay with it for five more minutes because you're not dead yet. Persistence is more important than talent. It gives you a chance when nothing else will.

Hit your goal, and then set one more for yourself.

Work through Stress

The paralyzing fear of overwhelming to-do lists and responsibilities can be suffocating. Deadlines, finances, budget, and personal life all carry a weight of seriousness that can pile up and become too heavy to bear at times. This stress comes as a result of our mind being focused away from the present moment and our work. The relief is in the work.

There is a way to motivate yourself through these times. The key is taking the action you are thinking about, which allows you to take advantage of time. Do the most important things first. Remember, the way work gets done is by somebody doing it, not by talking, analyzing, or worrying about it.

Try not to overthink that phone call or conversation you need to have. When you start going too far into your mind, running down side streets and rabbit trails, it's time to make the call or go have the conversation. It doesn't have to be perfectly planned. The words will come to you.

Take action to make things happen. Be confident in your ability to calm—or at least weather—a storm, to find a resolution. Then do the next thing on your list.

Dealing with Boredom

Keep hacking away at it, and find that loophole, that loose brick, or that moment of inspiration. You'll find it by continuing to show up and try different angles. There's an angle—it may only be a "good enough" angle—that will bring clarity and renewed energy for the task. It only comes through doing. Don't give in to boredom.

Warren Buffett established his investing strategy early in life based on numerous readings of the book *Security Analysis* by Benjamin Graham. This is a tedious read, and I have not read anywhere that Buffett himself necessarily enjoyed reading it. But he read it over and over and became extremely successful with what some would consider his boring approach to investing. So on the other hand, don't imagine that boredom is always bad or something to be overcome. It can be accepted. We don't need to be wildly inspired or full of passion to create something or to work on our goal.

Another strategy for dealing with boredom is to give yourself time limits. If you find yourself bored with a project, tell yourself you'll work on it for five more minutes. When those five minutes have passed, try another five. This can work as a hack to get you back into it, and maybe ten, twenty, or thirty minutes go by before you look up from your work again.

What else can you do with boredom?

We can beat boredom by the simplest of actions. Taking a walk, writing notes, doing push-ups, making a list, reading a book, and watching a movie; all can help us overcome the feeling of boredom.

When you are faced with anxiety or boredom, do. Imagine you are in a prison. We all have our own prisons, metaphorically speaking. What can you do within the cell you are in? There's something there that you can do in the moment that will allow you to shake the feelings of boredom and get back to your work.

More Action, Fewer Regrets

There are many ways to take action. Some action could be escapism and could result in negative consequences to our lives and goals while other forms of action bring positive results. There are no step-by-step instructions here. The only thing to do is that which brings us closer to our goals, that which aligns most closely with the purpose we have for our life.

There's a good chance that whatever it is that we don't want to do, whatever it is that we are worrying about, whatever it is that we are putting off, procrastinating, dreading, and sweating—that is the thing we should do. Do it. When we do it, we will be surprised by the sudden and remarkable clarity of mind we have afterward.

This is because we are in line with our purpose. We are not trying to find a shortcut, an escape, a way to someone else's life and purpose. Instead, we are sticking to our own path, journey, and adventure. This is critical in discovering who we are and moving past the obstacles of mind that pin us down as if holding us under water. Feelings of boredom are a result of letting the mind lose focus on our purpose and turning away from what we know is the right action for the time.

And when I say time, I mean right now. I've heard it said that the mind takes about five seconds to pick one action or another when in doubt. I don't know if that is scientifically or neurologically accurate, but it seems correct when viewed in light of my own experience.

For example, I can plan all day to go home and exercise in the evening, but on the way home after a long day at the office, a cold six-pack of beer is more appealing. Driving, I have a matter of seconds upon approaching the convenience store whether to keep driving or stop, and the decision is made one way or the other that fast. Another example is when I am planning to do some writing. When I sit down at the computer, I have a matter of seconds to decide whether to open the document and start writing, or to click on the search engine and watch YouTube.

We have an opportunity to make a choice each moment, and either we make choices that bring us closer to our goal, closer to who we are and what we were meant to be doing in this experience of consciousness, or we make a choice that brings regret and boredom and discontent that follows us until we get back on our path.

So in order to get that weight off our mind, we need to let go and just take the action. It will follow that our mental state will change from depression to a sense of productivity and achievement. Remember this the next time you feel the negative feelings discussed here, and you will be able to react with the proper action to replace the negativity with productivity.

Work through Negative Opinions

No matter how you find your motivation to live and create, you will always run into people who feel the need to criticize and voice their opinion. Most of the time, they are wrong. In any case, their opinions of you do not matter. But especially at first, guard your goal. Be careful about who you share your goals with so that you don't invite negativity unnecessarily.

People's opinions of you are nothing but the wind blowing; today it blows east, tomorrow it blows west.

Stay wholly focused on the work and on the quality of the work. Check your motivations. If you're doing it to make someone like you, it's not good quality. Don't attach much importance to others' reactions to work you've undertaken with authentic motives. Only trust your motives and the quality of the work because you can't control or trust others' reactions.

Remember, not everyone likes you, and it doesn't matter who and it doesn't matter why. You just be you. Other authentic people will confront you if there is a problem. You can't help the phonies, so you've got no reason to be overly concerned about offending people.

Without fail, the second you start feeling good about yourself because of others' encouragement or good opinion, someone else appears to knock you down a peg with their own opinion or label.

Opinions, good and bad, change too easily to be relied upon. Keep hustling. Do more work.

Procrastination

I mentioned *The War of Art* by Steven Pressfield in an earlier chapter. In his book, he talks about what he calls "Resistance," which is anything that prevents us from doing our work. Basically, it keeps us from expressing ourselves fully in the universe. It manifests itself in many forms, and procrastination is one of them. Pressfield describes it this way:

"Procrastination is the most common manifestation of Resistance because it's the easiest to rationalize. We don't tell ourselves 'I'm never going to write my symphony.' Instead we say, 'I am going to write my symphony; I am just going to start tomorrow.'"

What are you putting off until tomorrow? Can you start it today?

Procrastination itself takes many forms too. It is easy to deceive ourselves into thinking we are working or planning or researching when we are in fact consuming others' work while searching for a source of motivation or inspiration. Or we are collaborating, but we are really looking for someone else to provide the spark to get us moving. Great things aren't always accomplished by groups of people; many times, great success is driven by the efforts and persistence of the solitary individual. Don't wait for help or inspiration—get to work. Work will provide the inspiration; it's not the other way around.

Create your own motivation. This is your why. Some people use visual tactics like creating a dream board or a vision board that has pictures representing their goals. Whatever it takes to motivate you, do that. Begin work now and save yourself from regret later. Countless hours are wasted talking about what we could do or what we would do or hundreds of other ideas.

Many versions of personal success disappear due to procrastination and tomorrow never coming. Focus on your goal and make the work priority. You'll sleep better this way.

In the next chapter, we'll talk about sharing with others the steps that work for us and lessons we have learned along our path.

CHAPTER SEVEN

SHARE YOUR JOURNEY

People in the same boat should help each other.
—CHINESE SAYING

As we continue on our journey to personal success, it is beneficial to ourselves and others to share our story. Now is the time to open yourself up to the world and make connections. Developing relationships based on respect, hard work, and mutual help and encouragement is crucial to finding satisfaction in life and reaching your personal success goal.

I encourage you to look forward to meeting people. For some of us, this might be outside of our comfort zone, but it is a discomfort that should be faced and overcome for the benefits. Start small. Start by getting to know someone at work that you never really talk to. Or you could start by talking to your neighbor once in a while or the clerk at the store you frequent. If you take small steps, you can begin to enjoy meeting and talking to people, and from there, you can be strategic in reaching out to people and connecting with others in your industry that could become mentors or collaborators. But first, put yourself out there.

People keep their heads down and avoid eye contact at all cost. We miss out on so many connections, and possibly even friendships, due to the awkwardness of a moment. Embrace the awkwardness. Learn to work through it. You will be amazed at the connections you make. It's often a numbers game in life, and this is a good example. If you attempt to talk to ten people, and seven of them are overcome by the awkwardness or are full of their own thoughts and emotions or simply have no desire to connect with you, that still leaves three connections you made by being awkward (human) enough to connect. It is worth it.

Introverts Included

Maybe you're an introvert. If you would rather be alone nine times out of ten, if you prefer one-on-one interaction to group activities, if you look for excuses to avoid social gatherings and get anxious before going to them, you are commonly labeled as an introvert. Here's a secret: while there is truth to the notion that you prefer your own company to most everyone else you know, you are not necessarily incapable of being a social person.

Practice listening to others. You'll find plenty to talk about if you listen and ask questions based on what you hear. It is a quick way to become likable in conversation as most people like to tell their story and like to be heard. Make yourself comfortable around this truth and get to know people. There is much to be learned, much to be gained, by hearing other people's stories. Not always, but often. Don't let a few bad experiences turn you off from people altogether.

Dale Carnegie, in his highly effective book, *How to Win Friends and Influence People*, puts it this way: "You can make more friends in two months by becoming interested in other people than you can in two years by trying to get other people interested in you." And by adapting this strategy, you will coincidentally become more interesting yourself as you learn more about communication, hear more stories, and gain more practice interacting with other human beings. You'll learn their tendencies, likes, and dislikes, and you'll gradually start applying this knowledge to future engagements and encounters, and before you know it, you will start looking forward to meeting people.

On their deathbed, people regret losing the friendships and relationships as they die. They say connections with other humans, not money or possessions, is what matters at the end. Human interaction usually brings pleasure, and plenty of paranoia and anxiety comes from feeling and being alone. Friendship is the answer.

Mentors, Master Mind Groups, Collaboration

Another way in which being social and getting to know others is a benefit is that you can find people within your industry or field of interest and become friends, trade ideas, ask questions, learn from each other, and grow based on shared wisdom. Napoleon Hill in his book, *Think and Grow Rich*, introduced the idea of a Master Mind group. He likened the power of a group of minds to battery power.

"It is a well-known fact that a group of electric batteries will provide more energy than a single battery. It is also a well-known fact that an individual battery will provide energy in proportion to the number and capacity of the cells it contains.

"The brain functions in a similar fashion. This accounts for the fact that some brains are more efficient than others, and leads to this significant statement—a group of brains coordinated (or connected) in a spirit of harmony, will provide more thought-energy than a single brain, just as a group of electric batteries will provide more energy than a single battery."

With the internet, it is easier than ever before in history to create these groups of human minds to solve problems, to encourage each other, and to work to produce more energy than one mind would be able to on its own. There are many different ways to make this happen, and it is useful to try to create a circle of people around you or in your contacts that you can trust your goals and your ideas and that will give you useful feedback and answers to critical questions.

Ask for Help

Each of us has unique skill sets, strengths, and weaknesses. It is wise to reach out to others and ask for help and collaboration to maximize our full potential. Some of us are good at artistic pursuits in life, some are good at marketing, some at sales, and others at financial savviness. Know thyself. What are you good at and what are your weaknesses? Get help in the weak spots of your endeavors, and spend most of your own time on your strengths. This is how you will reach your personal success goals.

We are proud: we let our ego get the best of us, and we refuse to ask for help. This is a critical mistake in self-awareness, and it delays—and sometimes stops altogether—our journey to personal success. Enlist help by offering your skills and time in exchange. When we help each other, we all win.

Sharing Your Personal Story Empowers Others

As you open up and share with others, you may be surprised to learn that you have helped someone who heard your story, who had a particular problem or need that something you said helped them with. You never know. Why keep everything to yourself? Put the knowledge you gained from your personal success journey out there where it can be of value to others. Everyone you meet has problems you don't know about, so let's try to be more kind. Let's try to be encouraging along our journey with everyone we meet.

With the internet and smartphones, it is easier than ever before to share stories and information with people we have never met. Think about your life story and the events in your life that might be useful to share. What obstacles have you successfully overcome in your life? What parts of your journey could you share with others that might help them in their own life? What do you wish you would have known when you went through a difficult time in your life? Can you share that knowledge with others who may someday go through the same hard times?

Owning and telling your story can be a powerful step in your personal development.

Accept Your Need To Fit In

No matter what, we will always care what other people think. The person who says "I don't care what anyone thinks of me" still needs others to think one way or the other. He needs those people in order to show them "he doesn't care what they think."

While it's useful to realize the meaninglessness of others' opinions when it comes to pursuing your goal, it's a losing battle to try to get to an imagined point of not caring what others think. We long for acceptance among other people.

We mistakenly look at the world as separate from ourselves. While we have our unique DNA, we are all still part of this one phenomenon that we call life. Because of the way our minds function, we divide and categorize and label and eventually see ourselves as different from others to varying degrees. We see ourselves as extremely different and separate from the person who is the opposite sex and lives on the other side of the world, and only slightly different than our biological brother or sister or best friend.

In fact, we are not so different. We are all experiencing consciousness; we are all born into a set of circumstances outside of our control and in spite of the incredible odds of not being born at all. We are brought up in whatever family, religion, city, country, and continent that we happen to be born into, and we are conscious of this experience from the perspective of our own minds.

If you are fortunate enough to have been born into a country where you are free to choose your circumstances more purposefully as you grow into adulthood, take full advantage of this. Most importantly, spread positivity to all people regardless of differences, real or imagined.

We are born and we die, and our consciousness of these facts is what we all have in common. It is natural for us to find comfort in sharing with and relating to others aboard this ship we call life. As we begin to see each other as a human race, rather than all of the different divisions we have made up over the centuries, we can behave toward each other with kindness. Understanding that we are in the same boat let us act out of love rather than hatred or competitiveness, which grows out of a mistaken sense of division.

In Closing

We provide additional value by telling our story to others around us and empowering them to start or continue on their own journey. We help ourselves as individuals when we help each other.

Practice patience. In the internet age, we expect things to happen quickly as we grow accustomed to the

exponentially increasing speed of technological progress. Patience is required in mastering the mind, and
mental control—to be able to control our perspective, attention, and actions—is the ultimate goal. If
you've read this book, you are already thinking about
the idea of changing your life circumstances. That is
the first step—to believe it is possible.

You can find your own version of success. Not every
answer will be given to you, but if you are willing to
look within—to hold up a mirror to the self you think
you know—and to act on what you learn, you will
discover how the mind can be persuaded and your life
changed.

When you become who you are, embrace and accept
your flaws and strengths, then begin working toward
aligning what you do and what you want to do, all the
success you dream of will follow you. It will follow the
action you take.

As you assess your life and learn more about yourself,
be forgiving. If you don't overcome fears as quickly as
you would like, give yourself grace. There is no room

for judging yourself on this journey because that will only hold you back. The cliché about the journey being the best part is true, but there are ups and downs. Be conscious of the experience, and you will see the signs that will help you when you are stuck—if you are patient.

When you are starting out, there may not be much to be positive about, but with each step forward toward your goal, you will see progress, and your confidence and optimism will increase. The momentum will begin to shift. You will start to see that you do have what it takes to be what you want to be, and this will motivate you to do more. Undoubtedly, you will face downtimes where you second guess your decisions, procrastinate, and experience personal pain and loss. When this happens, remember to stay present and allow the sadness or frustration to pass.

Life is cyclical, and you will feel energized and ready to get back into the work soon enough. Keep moving forward and enjoying the process and remember to share what you're learning with others!

ACKNOWLEDGMENTS

Thanks to...

Mom and Dad for instilling patience and work ethic; Heather, Riley, and Kaden for love and laughter; Nathan Martin for introducing me to the genre; Dave Wildasin for giving me a shot; Annmarie Steffes for strong edits; Eileen Rockwell for an awesome cover design; Susan Ramundo for the excellent page design; and to my friends and family for your support and love.

ABOUT THE AUTHOR

John Martin enjoys writing, reading, and study-
ing personal development and human psychology.
Empower Yourself is his first book.